M·A·R·K 12™
Reading

Activity Book

Volume I

Book Staff and Contributors

Kristen Kinney *Senior Content Specialist*
Amy Rauen *Instructional Designer*
David Shireman *Instructional Designer*
Michelle Iwaszuk *Instructional Designer*
Kandee Dyczko *Writer*
Tisha Ruibal *Writer*
Julie Philpot *Editor*
Suzanne Montazer *Creative Director*
Sasha Blanton *Senior Print Designer, Cover Designer*
Julie Jankowski *Print Designer*
Stephanie Shaw *Illustrator*
Chris Franklin *Illustrator*
Matt Fedor *Illustrator*
Michelle Beauregard *Project Manager*
Carrie Miller *Project Manager*

John Holdren *Senior Vice President for Content and Curriculum*
Maria Szalay *Senior Vice President for Product Development*
David Pelizzari *Vice President of Content and Curriculum*
Kim Barcas *Vice President of Creative Design*
Seth Herz *Director, Program Management*

Lisa Dimaio Iekel *Production Manager*
John G. Agnone *Director of Publications*

About K12 Inc.

K12 Inc., a technology-based education company, is the nation's leading provider of proprietary curriculum and online education programs to students in grades K–12. K[12] provides its curriculum and academic services to online schools, traditional classrooms, blended school programs, and directly to families. K12 Inc. also operates the K[12] International Academy, an accredited, diploma-granting online private school serving students worldwide. K[12]'s mission is to provide any child the curriculum and tools to maximize success in life, regardless of geographic, financial, or demographic circumstances. K12 Inc. is accredited by CITA. More information can be found at www.K12.com.

978-1-60153-108-7

Printed by RR Donnelley, Willard, Ohio, USA, April 2016, Lot 042016

Contents

Sound Work and Sight Words

Sounds for Letters and Sight Words

Short Vowels and Sight Words

Digraphs and Sight Words

Long Vowels and Sight Words

Ending Blends and Sight Words

Beginning Blends and Sight Words

Word Endings and Sight Words

Difficult Spellings & r-Controlled Vowels and Sight Words

oi/*oy* and Sight Words

au/*aw* and Sight Words

Long *u* and Syllable Types

Long *u* & Double *o* and Syllable Types

Double *o* and Syllable Types

Schwa and Syllable Types

M·A·R·K 12™
Reading

Volume I

Name:

Letters

1. ________
2. ________
3. ________
4. ________
5. ________
6. ________
7. ________
8. ________
9. ________
10. ________
11. ________
12. ________
13. ________
14. ________
15. ________
16. ________
17. ________
18. ________
19. ________
20. ________
21. ________
22. ________
23. ________
24. ________
25. ________
26. ________

Sight Word Practice

1. ___________
2. ___________
3. ___________

4. s, i ___________
5. d, n, a ___________
6. h, e, t ___________

7. the
8. is
9. and

Get Ready

- There are four kinds of **sentences** that have different jobs.

  statements
  questions
  commands
  exclamations

Remember, a sentence is a group of words that expresses a complete thought. A sentence always starts with a capital letter. A sentence always ends with the appropriate punctuation mark. How do you know what kind of punctuation? It depends on the type of sentence.

- **Statements** are telling sentences and end with a period.

  I like candy.

- **Questions** are asking sentences and end with a question mark.

  Do you like candy?

- **Commands** tell what to do and end with a period.

  Eat your dinner.

- **Exclamations** express strong emotion and end with an exclamation mark.

  You did great work today!

Try It

Draw a line from each sentence type to the appropriate punctuation.

command	?
exclamation	.
question	.
statement	!

Listen as each sentence is read to you. Write the appropriate punctuation at the end of each sentence.

1. Sit down and talk to me
2. What movie did you go to see
3. That sounds exciting
4. I would like to see that movie, too

Name:

Sound Work and Sight Words 2

Listen for Rhymes

1. ____________________
2. ____________________
3. ____________________
4. ____________________
5. ____________________
6. ____________________
7. ____________________
8. ____________________
9. ____________________
10. ____________________

Missing Letters

A	____	____	n
____	b	____	o
____	c	____	p
____	d	____	q
E	____	R	____
F	____	S	____
G	____	T	____
____	h	____	u
I	____	____	v
J	____	____	w
____	k	____	x
____	l	Y	____
____	m	Z	____

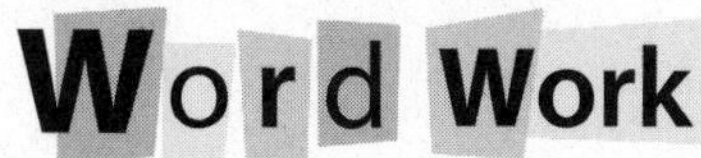

Name:

Sight Words: Spell and Check

Listen and Write	Read	Cover and Write	Check

Sight Words Practice

1. is
2. and
3. the

4. ______________
5. ______________
6. ______________

Listen for Sounds

1. ________
2. ________
3. ________
4. ________
5. ________
6. ________
7. ________
8. ________
9. ________
10. ________

Name:

Sound Work and Sight Words 3

Sight Words Practice

1. __________
2. __________
3. __________
4. __________
5. __________
6. __________

7. ot __________
8. ni __________
9. no __________
10. si __________
11. dna __________
12. het __________

13. to
14. is
15. the
16. on
17. and
18. in

Name:

Sound Chains

1.			
2.			
3.			
4.			
5.			
6.			
7.			
8.			
9.			
10.			
11.			
12.			

Name:

Counting Syllables

1. ______________________
2. ______________________
3. ______________________
4. ______________________
5. ______________________
6. ______________________
7. ______________________
8. ______________________
9. ______________________
10. ______________________
11. ______________________
12. ______________________

Word Search

the	to	on	and	is	in

i	s	b	o	n
j	t	h	e	z
q	v	x	k	m
t	o	h	i	n
a	n	d	w	r

Name:

Sound Work and Sight Words 4

Dictation

1. ______________
2. ______________
3. ______________
4. ______________
5. ______________
6. ______________

Counting Sounds

1. ____________________
2. ____________________
3. ____________________
4. ____________________
5. ____________________
6. ____________________
7. ____________________
8. ____________________
9. ____________________
10. ____________________
11. ____________________
12. ____________________

Sight Words

the	on	it
in	and	he
is	it	in
was	to	and
on	the	was
to	he	is

Time for first round: ________

Time for second round: ________

Get Ready

- All sentences have **subjects**. Let's learn what subjects are.

  A sentence is a group of words that expresses a complete thought. A sentence always starts with a *capital letter*. A sentence always ends with the appropriate *punctuation mark*. A sentence always contains a *subject*. The subject of a sentence tells the person, place, or thing the sentence is about.

- To identify the subject of the sentence, it may help to ask, "Who is this sentence about?" or, "What is the sentence about?"

  Avery is late again! *Who* is the sentence about? Avery. The subject of the sentence is *Avery*.

  The capital of the United States of America is Washington, DC. *What* is the sentence about? The capital. The subject of the sentence is *capital*.

  Remember: All sentences have a subject. The subject identifies the person, place, or thing that the sentence is about.

Name:

Try It

Listen as each sentence is read to you. Underline the subject in each sentence. Remember, a subject names the person, place, or thing that the sentence is about.

1. The bluebird perched on the birdhouse.
2. Brady was sick yesterday.
3. Jasper is friends with me.
4. The firemen rushed to the burning building.
5. The troop leader said we would camp out next month.
6. Sarah helped Mom pack.
7. The bike has a flat tire.
8. That lamp needs a new light bulb.
9. Can I have a tissue, please?
10. Jake and I are going to the movies.
11. The waitress brought us our desserts.
12. Dad went to the library without me!

Listening for Sounds

1.			
2.			
3.			
4.			
5.			
6.			
7.			
8.			
9.			
10.			
11.			
12.			

Sounds in Words

Ex.	X	X	X	X	X	
1.						
2.						
3.						
4.						
5.						
6.						

Sight Words Search

the	on	it
and	to	he
is	in	was

k	w	a	s	q	o	n	j	t
r	x	z	h	m	w	d	p	h
y	p	d	j	p	f	t	l	e
a	w	v	i	s	k	o	b	q
n	r	f	d	g	y	g	h	j
d	i	t	w	f	k	p	h	e
b	g	r	z	q	i	n	d	y

Name:

Sight Words Scramble

1. a w s ____________

2. e t h ____________

3. d n a ____________

4. n o ____________

5. o t ____________

6. t i ____________

7. e h ____________

8. n i ____________

Name:

Sound Work and Sight Words 7

Same or Different?

	Same	Different
1.	______	______
2.	______	______
3.	______	______
4.	______	______
5.	______	______
6.	______	______
7.	______	______
8.	______	______
9.	______	______
10.	______	______

Sight Words: Spell and Check

Listen and Write	Read	Cover and Write	Check

Unit 1 Assessment

Part 1.

1. the
2. and
3. is
4. on
5. to
6. in
7. it
8. he
9. was
10. says
11. have
12. with

Part 2.

13. ______
14. ______
15. ______
16. ______
17. ______
18. ______
19. ______
20. ______

Name:

Part 3.

21. ______
22. ______
23. ______
24. ______
25. ______
26. ______
27. ______
28. ______

Part 4.

29. ____________
30. ____________
31. ____________
32. ____________
33. ____________
34. ____________
35. ____________
36. ____________

Part 5.

	Same	Different
37.	______	______
38.	______	______
39.	______	______
40.	______	______
41.	______	______
42.	______	______
43.	______	______
44.	______	______
45.	______	______
46.	______	______
47.	______	______
48.	______	______

Part 6.

49. ______________

50. ______________

51. ______________

52. ______________

53. ______________

54. ______________

55. ______________

56. ______________

57. ______________

58. ______________

59. ______________

60. ______________

Beginning Letters

Listen to each word that is read to you. Mark the column of the letter that begins each word.

	a	b	f	m	s	t
1.						
2.						
3.						
4.						
5.						
6.						
7.						
8.						
9.						
10.						
11.						
12.						

Listen to each word that is read to you. Write each word on the lines provided.

13. ________ 14. ________ 15. ________ 16. ________

Name:

Sounds for Letters and Sight Words 1

Sight Words

Listen to each word that is read to you. Write each word on the lines provided.

1. ______________
2. ______________
3. ______________
4. ______________
5. ______________
6. ______________

Unscramble each sight word. Write each unscrambled sight word on the lines provided.

7. a, s, w ______________
8. e, h ______________
9. t, i ______________
10. e, e, h, r, t ______________
11. o, f, m, r ______________
12. e, e, h, r, w ______________

Read each word aloud. Say each word in a sentence.

13. in
14. there
15. to
16. from
17. on
18. where

Get Ready

- A sentence is a group of words that expresses a complete thought and contains both a subject and a predicate. The **predicate** of a sentence contains the verb and tells more about what the subject is or does. Look at this sentence:

  Mrs. Jones knows everyone on our street.

In this sentence, the subject is *Mrs. Jones*. To find the predicate, ask, "What does the sentence tell about the subject?"

  The predicate is *knows everyone on our street*.

Remember: All sentences have a predicate. The predicate of a sentence contains the verb and tells more about what the subject is or does.

Try It

Read each sentence. Underline the predicate in each sentence.

1. Matt threw the ball.
2. Mom drove to work.
3. That shirt fits Sam perfectly.
4. The taxi driver honked the horn.
5. My little brother draws very well.
6. The black cat jumped onto the bed.
7. My big sister likes to sing and dance.
8. My father plays the clarinet in a jazz band.
9. The big old branch cracked in the ice storm.
10. My friend runs faster than anyone else I know.

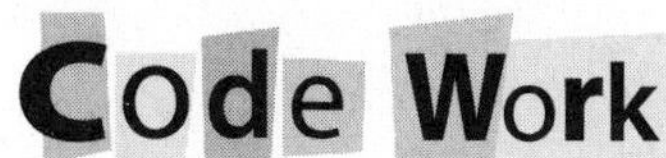

Name:

Sounds for Letters and Sight Words 2

Sounds and Letters

Listen to each sound that is read to you. On the lines provided, write the letter that makes each sound.

1. ________
2. ________
3. ________
4. ________
5. ________
6. ________
7. ________
8. ________
9. ________
10. ________
11. ________
12. ________
13. ________
14. ________
15. ________
16. ________
17. ________
18. ________

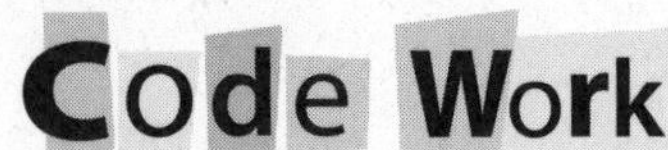

Name:

Sounds for Letters and Sight Words 2

Complete the Word

Listen to each word that is read to you. On the lines provided, write the missing letter in each word.

1. ______ab
2. pa______
3. ______am
4. ______at
5. ca______
6. ______at
7. ______ap
8. pa______
9. na______
10. ca______

Name:

Best Pick

Read each sentence aloud. Circle the word that best completes each sentence. Read each sentence aloud again to be sure it makes sense.

1. The dog is ______________.	hot	map
2. Sam ran a ______________.	lap	pal
3. Bob got a ______________.	gap	job
4. The cat is ______________.	cap	fat
5. Dad had a ______________.	mop	sat
6. Mom is on the ______________.	hop	mat
7. Dan got in the ______________.	pop	van
8. Pam and Jan pat the ______________.	cat	pan

Name:

Sounds for Letters and Sight Words 3

By Sight

See how many words you can read correctly in one minute. Read aloud across the rows. When you get to the bottom of the page, start over. Try to read more words the second time.

and	from	have	in
of	put	says	that
was	of	put	that
he	is	on	the
where	it	there	with

Number of words read correctly: ______

Sounds for Letters and Sight Words 3

Get Ready

- What **punctuation mark** is used at the end of a sentence? It depends on what kind of sentence it is. There are four kinds of sentences:

 statements
 questions
 commands
 exclamations

Statements tell something. They end in a period.

 I am in my room.

Questions ask for information. They end in a question mark.

 What are you doing?

Commands give an order or an instruction. They usually end in a period, but if they express strong emotion, they might also end in an exclamation point.

 Hurry up. *or* Hurry up!

Exclamations express strong emotion. They end in an exclamation point.

 That spider is huge!

Name:

Try It

Each sentence below is missing its end punctuation. Decide if each sentence is a statement, command, question, or exclamation. Write the missing punctuation marks on the lines provided.

1. Is this your cat ____
2. Where did you find her ____
3. I found her in my yard ____
4. She is so cute ____
5. Pick her up ____

On the lines provided below, write one statement, one command, one question, and one exclamation. Remember to end each sentence with the correct punctuation mark.

6. ______________________________

   ____

7. ______________________________

   ____

8. ______________________________

   ____

9. ______________________________

   ____

Word Chains

Read the first word aloud. One letter has been changed to make the next word. Circle the letter in each word below that has been changed. Then read the word aloud. The first one has been done for you.

r a n
(v) a n
c a n
c a p
n a p
l a p
z a p
z i p
t i p
d i p
d i g
d i m

h i m
h i d
k i d
k i t
b i t
s i t
p i t
p o t
d o t
d o g
j o g

Name:

Dictation

Listen to each word that is read to you. Write each word on the lines provided.

1. ____________
2. ____________
3. ____________
4. ____________
5. ____________
6. ____________
7. ____________
8. ____________
9. ____________
10. ____________

Name:

Sounds for Letters and Sight Words 4

Sight Words

Listen as each word is read to you. Write the word in the first column. Read the word aloud. After you read the word, place a check mark in the second column. Cover the word, and try to write it again in the third column. Uncover the word and check your spelling. If you wrote it correctly, place a check in the fourth column.

Listen and Write	Read	Cover and Write	Check

Word Search

Read each word in the box aloud. Circle each word in the word search below. Words may appear left to right or up and down.

and	have	from	is	of	put
says	that	was	on	the	to

s	o	w	y	a	z	x	v	t
a	n	d	p	h	a	v	e	k
b	d	f	h	i	g	e	c	s
f	r	o	m	z	i	s		a
j	l	f	p	q	o	m	k	y
a	c	e	g	p	u	t	d	s
s	u	w	y	z	x	h	t	r
t	h	a	t	q	o	e	k	i
b	d	s	h	t	o	e	c	a

Name:

Sounds for Letters and Sight Words 5

Best Pick

Read each sentence aloud. Circle the word that best completes each sentence. Read each sentence aloud again to be sure it makes sense.

1.	The __________ is hot.	wax	wet
2.	The __________ has a lid.	box	bun
3.	I can __________ to the van.	rat	run
4.	The dog is in the __________.	map	mud
5.	The __________ has six kids in it.	bat	bus

Word Scramble

Unscramble the letters to create a word. Write each word on the lines provided. Then read the words aloud.

6. x f o ________________

7. n f u ________________

8. n t u ________________

9. g m u ________________

10. i n w ________________

Name:

Sight Words

Listen to each word that is read to you. Write each word on the lines provided.

1. ______________ 4. ______________

2. ______________ 5. ______________

3. ______________ 6. ______________

Unscramble each sight word. Write each unscrambled sight word on the lines provided.

7. e, h, y, t ______________ 10. e, e, h, r, t ______________

8. t, h, b, o ______________ 11. o, f, m, r ______________

9. p, t, u ______________ 12. o, t, w ______________

Read each word aloud. Say each word in a sentence.

13. both 16. they

14. he 17. two

15. says 18. with

Unit 2 Assessment

Part 1.

Say the sound each letter or letters make.

1. y	**6.** w	**11.** x	**16.** z	**21.** qu
2. v	**7.** k	**12.** g	**17.** d	**22.** r
3. p	**8.** n	**13.** l	**18.** h	**23.** j
4. c	**9.** f	**14.** b	**19.** m	**24.** s
5. t	**10.** w	**15.** z	**20.** x	**25.** y

Part 2.

Listen to each sound that is read to you. Circle the letter that makes each sound.

26. a e i o u	**35.** v w x y z	**44.** n p qu r s
27. v w x y z	**36.** c k qu s x	**45.** l m n p qu
28. c d qu s x	**37.** r s t v w	**46.** g h j k l
29. b c f g h	**38.** s t v w x	**47.** d f g h j
30. a e i o u	**39.** a e i o u	**48.** b c d f g
31. p qu r s t	**40.** f k qu s x	**49.** k l m n p
32. v w x y z	**41.** c d f g h	**50.** s t v w x
33. a e i o u	**42.** d j k l m	**51.** a e i o u
34. c k qu s x	**43.** f g h j k	

Name:

Sounds for Letters and Sight Words

Part 3.

Listen to each word that is read to you. Write the letter that is missing from each word in the blank space.

52. ______m

53. j______t

54. bi______

55. ______og

56. ______t

57. ______it

58. b______x

59. ______ed

60. ______s

61. ______an

Part 4.

Listen to each sound that is read to you. Say the letter that makes each sound. Write each letter on the lines provided.

62. ______

63. ______

64. ______

65. ______

66. ______

67. ______

68. ______

69. ______

70. ______

71. ______

Name:

Sounds for Letters and Sight Words

Part 5.

Listen to each word that is read to you. Write each word on the lines provided.

72. ________

73. ________

74. ________

75. ________

76. ________

77. ________

78. ________

79. ________

80. ________

81. ________

Part 6.

Read each word aloud.

82. two

83. both

84. they

85. from

86. there

87. of

88. put

89. that

90. where

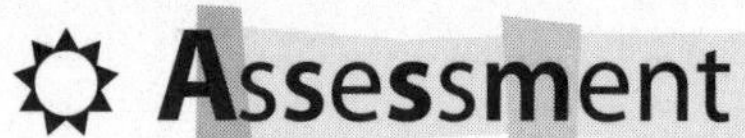

Name:

Sounds for Letters and Sight Words

Part 7.

In each row, underline the word that is read to you.

91.	the	there	they
92.	where	was	wet
93.	that	the	there
94.	pat	put	pet
95.	at	in	of
96.	the	there	they
97.	fan	fit	from
98.	bat	both	bit
99.	two	ten	top

Name:

Words with Short Vowels

Add or subtract a letter to make a new word. Write the new word on the line provided.

Example: f + at = fat

1. c + at = ________
2. t + ax = ________
3. pad – p = ________
4. r + an = ________
5. kit – k = ________
6. can – c = ________
7. p + in = ________
8. hat – h = ________
9. p + it = ________
10. ram – r = ________

Choose the word from the box that best completes each sentence. Write the word on the line provided.

fed	tin	pig	sad	hat	bed

11. Deb has a ________ can.
12. Pam has a red ________.
13. Tim sat on the ________.
14. Ted is ________.
15. The ________ had a nap.
16. Wes ________ the cat.

Name:

Short Vowels and Sight Words 1

Sight Word Work

Unscramble each sight word. Write the word on the line provided.

1. oyu ____________
2. eyht ____________
3. netw ____________
4. wot ____________
5. ew ____________
6. thob ____________

Choose the word from the box that best completes each sentence. Write the word on the line provided.

we	went	you

7. He ____________ home.
8. She gave one to ____________ and me.
9. He says ____________ can go, too.

Get Ready

Direct Quotations and Quotation Marks

When you quote a speaker's words exactly, it is called a **direct quotation**. The two sentences below have direct quotations.

> Henry asked, "Can you come over today, Jeff?"
>
> "Yes, I can!" said Jeff.

Notice that each sentence contains Henry's and Jeff's exact words, and their words are inside **quotation marks**. Remember that punctuation marks are like road signs for readers. Here, they signal someone's exact words are inside the quotation marks. Notice that the quotation marks enclose the end punctuation, too.

Commas in Direct Quotations

If the direct quotation comes at the end of the sentence, introduce it with a comma before the first set of quotation marks. End the direct quotation with the punctuation mark that fits the kind of sentence quoted. Put the punctuation mark before the second set of quotation marks.

> Henry said to Jeff, "Let's play football."

But if the direct quotation *starts a sentence*, you usually use a comma instead of a period at the end of it. Compare the sentence above to the sentence below. Notice how the punctuation changes from a period to a comma when the direct quotation is moved from the end to the beginning of the sentence.

> "Let's play football," Henry said to Jeff.

Some direct quotations use question marks or exclamation points, whether the quotation starts or ends the sentence.

> Jeff replied, "Can't we do something else?"
>
> "Sure! I'm sick of football, anyway!" Henry exclaimed.

Try It

Listen as two sentences with direct quotations are read to you. Write each sentence on the line provided. Be sure to use correct punctuation.

1. ______________________________

____

2. ______________________________

____

Underline the punctuation that shows Ned is asking a question in the following sentence.

3. Ben had to ask me, "Where is the cat?"

Underline the punctuation that shows Dad is shouting in the following sentence.

4. "Do not do that!" Dad says.

Unit 3 Assessment

Part 1.

Listen to each word that is read to you. Write the words on the lines provided.

1. ______________
2. ______________
3. ______________
4. ______________
5. ______________
6. ______________
7. ______________
8. ______________
9. ______________
10. ______________
11. ______________
12. ______________
13. ______________
14. ______________

Name:

Short Vowels and Sight Words

Part 2.

Underline the word that best completes each sentence. Then write the word on the line provided.

15.	The dog is in the ________.	rub	cub	tub
16.	Tom has a pot with a ________.	lad	lid	led
17.	We both had a can of ________.	pop	pep	pup
18.	The bug ran to the ________.	pat	fat	mat
19.	Dad went to ________ at six.	fed	bed	red
20.	Ron met me on the ________.	bus	bun	bud
21.	Pam went to her ________.	cob	rob	job
22.	You can ________ on that pad.	pit	sit	fit
23.	Hal put the ________ in the bag.	hum	gum	sum
24.	Ben ________ on the rug.	sat	sag	sad

Name:

Short Vowels and Sight Words

Part 3.

Read the story in the box. Then read each question. Write the answer to each question on the line provided.

Deb has a pet dog. Her dog is Bud. Deb can sit on the log. Bud can sit on the pad. Deb and Bud can run in the sun. Deb and Bud can have fun!

25. Who has a pet dog? ____________

26. What can Deb do on the log? ____________

27. Where can Bud sit? ____________

28. What can Deb and Bud do in the sun? ____________

29. What can Deb and Bud have? ____________

Part 4.

Listen to the word that is read to you. Find the word in the sentence. Underline the word.

30. Sam says you can have a hot dog.

31. The man went to the hut.

32. Can we run in the wet fog?

Name:

Short Vowels and Sight Words

Part 5.

Read each sentence. Find the word in the box that rhymes with the underlined word. Write that word on the line provided. An example has been done for you.
Hint: One word is not used.

box	vet	rug	run
rat	hat	ten	sit

Example: She is Pat. That is her rat .

33. I have a fox. It is in a ________.

34. Rex can quit. Then he can ________.

35. Where are the men? There are ________.

36. There is a bug. It is on the ________.

37. I have a pet. It is at the ________.

38. What a fun cat! It has a ________.

Part 6.

Listen to each word that is read to you. Write the words on the lines provided.

39. ________

40. ________

41. ________

Name:

Practice Digraphs

Write each word in the correct column below, according to the digraph found in each word.

sash	moth	ship	fish	thin	this
then	that	than	bath	path	shop

sh	***th***	***th***

Choose the word from the box that best completes each sentence. Write the word on the line provided.

the	shot	wish	math	thug	dash

1. Tim had to get a ____________ from Doctor Nash.
2. The ____________ ran from the cop.
3. I ____________ I had a pet dog.
4. This ____________ is fun!
5. Don had to ____________ to the bus.
6. Bob has ____________ mug.

Sight Word Search

Read the sight words in the box below. Find each word in the word search and circle it.

you	went	we	said	your	so

y	o	u	d	g	t	e	w	e
s	d	w	e	n	t	r	y	e
a	c	p	d	m	t	e	o	r
i	s	o	r	f	y	t	u	f
d	l	c	d	s	t	e	r	e
y	o	o	d	g	t	e	w	e

Complete the Sentence

Choose the words from the box that best complete each sentence. Write the words on the lines provided.

said	your	so

1. We ____________ no.
2. It was ____________ small.
3. I will put ____________ ball down.

Name:

Digraphs *ch* and *wh*

Read each sentence. Underline each word that has the digraph *ch* or the digraph *wh*.

1. Dan and Chad were on the bus.
2. Tom hit the can with a whip.
3. The van can chug up the path.
4. We went to the pet shop on a whim.
5. The ball hit Chip on the chin.
6. We can chat when I get there.

Choose the correct diagraph from the box and write the digraph on the line to make a word. Then say the word aloud.

ch	*wh*

Example: __ch__ in

7. ri__________
8. __________op
9. __________en
10. mu__________
11. __________iz
12. __________um
13. su__________
14. __________ere

Sight Words

Underline the sight word listed as many times as it appears in each row. An example has been done for you.

Example: the		<u>the</u>	that	<u>the</u>	it	that
1.	your	you	says	your	you	your
2.	you	you	your	you	your	you
3.	went	where	we	went	where	went
4.	we	we	went	where	we	we
5.	so	to	so	on	to	is
6.	said	says	said	and	said	says

Complete the Sentence

Choose the word from the box that best completes each sentence. Write each word on the line provided.

said	your	so

7. He is ____________ bad.

8. Mom ____________ no.

9. He has ____________ hat.

Chip and Chad

Chip and Chad sit on their log.

Chad has a jar of jam. Chip has a hot dog on a bun.

Chip and Chad have a chat.

"Is that hot dog good?" Chad says.

"It is good!" Chip says. "And is that jam good?" Chip says to Chad.

"It is good!" Chad says.

"You have a bit of jam on your chin," Chip says to Chad.

"Look at that!" says Chad.

"I have a rag," Chip says. "You can fix it."

"Yes, I can mop the jam from my chin with the rag," Chad says. "Look! No more jam on my chin!" Chad says to Chip. "That rag was good to have. You are a good chum!"

"And you are a good chap!" Chip says.

"What fun we have on our log," Chad says.

"You bet!" Chip says. Chad gets up.

"I want a nap," Chad says on a whim.

"Yes!" Chip says. "Let us have a nap!"

"We can nap on that pad," Chad says.

And with that, Chip and Chad have a nap on the pad.

© 2010 K12 Inc. All rights reserved.

Unit 4 Assessment

Part 1.

Listen to each word that is read to you. Underline the digraph or the trigraph that is in the word you hear.

1. ch ck sh tch th th wh
2. ch ck sh tch th th wh
3. ch ck sh tch th th wh
4. ch ck sh tch th th wh
5. ch ck sh tch th th wh
6. ch ck sh tch th th wh
7. ch ck sh tch th th wh
8. ch ck sh tch th th wh
9. ch ck sh tch th th wh
10. ch ck sh tch th th wh
11. ch ck sh tch th th wh
12. ch ck sh tch th th wh
13. ch ck sh tch th th wh
14. ch ck sh tch th th wh

Name:

Digraphs and Sight Words

Part 2.

Choose a word from the box and determine which digraph or trigraph is in the word. Write the word in the correct column.

whip	match	that	rash	rack	then	whiz
much	chip	tack	thug	thin	shop	latch

15. *ch*	16. *ck*	17. *sh*	18. *tch*

19. *th*	20. *th* (underlined)	21. *wh*

Part 3.

In each row, underline the word that has a digraph. Say the word aloud.

22. bash gum hut

23. den not whim

24. mop shut dug

25. yum gas moth

26. whip tan rap

27. fig mix this

☼ Assessment

Name:

Part 4.

In each row, underline the word that is read to you.

28. then their they

29. what was when

30. son so shop

31. sad said some

32. went win want

33. your or you

Part 5.

Choose the word from the box that best completes each sentence. Write the word on the line provided.
Hint: Two words in the box are not used.

went	so	both	want	what	your

34. Is that ______________ cup?

35. Tad ______________ to the pet shop.

36. I ______________ a red truck.

37. That cat is ______________ big!

Name:

Digraphs and Sight Words

Part 6.

Underline the letter in parentheses that completes each word. Write the completed word on the line provided. Then say the word aloud.

Example: bo_h (s, t, c) both

38. you_ (r, g, l) ____________

39. _o (s, f, w) ____________

40. wa_t (d, h, n) ____________

41. _aid (c, s, f) ____________

42. t_eir (e, r, h) ____________

43. wha_ (s, n, t) ____________

Name:

Digraphs and Sight Words 3

Get Ready

Nouns

A **noun** names a *person*, *place*, *thing*, or *idea*.

Here are some examples of nouns.

Persons: baker, dad, captain
Places: library, home, pond
Things: plate, cat, window
Ideas: freedom, sadness, love

A noun can tell *who* or *what*.

Who: man, baby, friend, kid, clown
What: garden, city, pencil, dog, happiness

Read the sentence below. Each underlined word is a noun.

The boy went to the zoo to watch the monkey for fun.

The boy is a *person*. The zoo is a *place*. The monkey is a *thing*. Having fun is an *idea*.

Interesting to know: The word **noun** is a noun! It names a *thing*.

Name:

Try It

Read each word in the box. Underline the word if it is a noun.

dog	run	they	when	sun
quick	shack	fetch	sash	where
tent	rich	cup	both	what

Read each sentence. Underline the noun or nouns in each sentence.

1. The girl found a pink shell on the sand.
2. She put it in her big bucket.
3. Suddenly the shell began to move!
4. There was a crab inside the shell!
5. The girl put the shell with the crab back on the sand.

Sorting Words by Vowel Sounds

Repeat each word after it is read to you. Listen for the vowel sound and write each word under the correct column for the vowel sound that you hear. Then write two more words for each vowel sound.

Short *a*	Long *a*	Short *e*	Long *e*

Name:

Long Vowels and Sight Words 1

Complete the Sentence

Choose the word from the box that best completes each sentence. Write the word on the line provided.

said	what	your	their	so	want

1. Tom and Mat lost ________________ dog.
2. You left ________________ bag at the mall.
3. This work is ________________ hard.
4. I did not see ________________ he did.
5. I ________________ a big lunch.
6. Dad ________________ you went to bed.

Sight Word Scramble

Unscramble each sight word and write it on the line provided.

7. rehit ________________
8. tahw ________________
9. natw ________________

"I had to run to the bus, but I made it!" Dale said to Kate.

Then they went to the lake and sat on the dock.

"I bet that the red ship can win!" Kate said.

"And I bet that the tan ship can win!" Dale said.

Dale and Kate had a fun date!

The Date

Dale was late. He had a date with Kate, and he was late.

Dale ran to the gate.

"I am so late!" Dale said. "I hate to be late!"

Dale went by Shane.

"What is your rush?" Shane said.

"I am late for my date with Kate," Dale said. "I want to take her to the ship race at the lake."

"I bet you have to run to catch the bus," Shane said.

"Yes!" Dale said. "I have to run as quick as I can!"

Dale ran up the path. He ran and ran.

Dale made a dash for the bus when it came. He made it!

"I got on the bus! I am not late!" Dale said as he sat on the bus.

Kate met Dale when he got off the bus.

"You are not late!" Kate said to Dale.

Unit 5 Assessment

Part 1.

Read each word below. On the line provided, write *Y* (for *yes*) if the word has a long vowel sound. Write *N* (for *no*) if the word does not have a long vowel sound.

1. bike ______
2. cake ______
3. dash ______
4. Eve ______
5. fetch ______
6. this ______
7. zone ______
8. bone ______
9. cube ______
10. tuck ______

Name:

Long Vowels and Sight Words

Part 2.

Listen to each word that is read to you. Write the word on the line provided.

11. ______________

12. ______________

13. ______________

14. ______________

15. ______________

16. ______________

17. ______________

18. ______________

19. ______________

20. ______________

Name:

Long Vowels and Sight Words

Part 3.

In each row, underline the word that contains a long vowel sound.

21.	chop	chase	check
22.	den	dive	dog
23.	fume	fan	fed
24.	mash	met	mute
25.	Pete	Pam	Peg
26.	thick	top	take
27.	whole	wax	wet
28.	cash	cone	cup
29.	that	thin	these
30.	time	tag	ten

Name:

Long Vowels and Sight Words

Part 4.

In each row, underline the word that is read to you.

31.	said	so	or
32.	said	your	so
33.	who	see	or
34.	your	so	see
35.	said	see	or
36.	who	see	so
37.	said	who	or
38.	said	your	so
39.	who	see	or
40.	so	who	your
41.	said	see	or
42.	your	so	who

Part 5.

Read each word aloud.

43. said
44. your
45. so
46. who
47. see
48. or
49. so
50. said
51. or
52. who
53. your
54. see

Get Ready

- A **noun** is a *person*, *place*, *thing*, or *idea*. Here are some examples of nouns:

  Persons: carpenter, parent, Mayor Ruiz

  Places: library, New York, pond

  Things: plate, Statue of Liberty, window

  Ideas: freedom, sadness, liberty

- Take a look at these two nouns:

  city

  Chicago

We call *city* a **common noun**. Common nouns tell about a *general* group or kind of person, place, or thing.

Chicago names a particular city. We call *Chicago* a **proper noun**. Proper nouns name a *particular* person, place, or thing. Proper nouns are *capitalized*.

Common Nouns	Proper Nouns
man	Mr. Davis
city	Jacksonville
team	Lakers
state	Kansas
holiday	Thanksgiving
ocean	Pacific Ocean
author	E.B. White

Name:

Try It

Underline the common nouns in the box. Circle the proper nouns.

run	bag	Dan
fade	gave	hat
Denver	sadness	sit
rock	bake	Sarah
freedom	made	Boston

Write each noun from the box above in the correct column below. Then write one more word of your own in each column.

Person	Place	Thing	Idea

Ending Blends

Draw a line from two beginning letters to an ending blend to make a word. Write the word on the line. Then read each word aloud. The first one has been done for you.

1. ra ct raft
2. bu ft ______
3. fa nd ______
4. be lk ______

Add beginning letters to each ending blend to create a word.

Example: se nd

5. ______ct
6. ______ft
7. ______nd
8. ______lk

Name:

Ending Blends and Sight Words 1

Sight Words

Underline the sight word listed as many times as it appears in each row. An example has been done for you.

Example: on	on	in	on	is	in	
1. or	to	so	or	your	or	
2. see	see	so	see	he	see	
3. who	to	with	who	went	who	

Sight Word Search

Read the sight words in the box below. Find each word in the word search and circle it.

what	their	who	see	or	want

y	o	t	w	h	a	t	w	r
s	d	h	t	w	a	n	t	e
s	c	e	d	m	t	e	o	r
e	s	i	r	w	h	o	u	f
e	l	r	e	s	t	d	r	e

Fog, fog, fog! The cub can hop in the fog.

Log, log, log! The cub can jog to the log.

Bug, Bug, Bug!

Bug, bug, bug! Rob has a big, fat bug.

Rug, rug, rug! Rob put the bug on the rug.

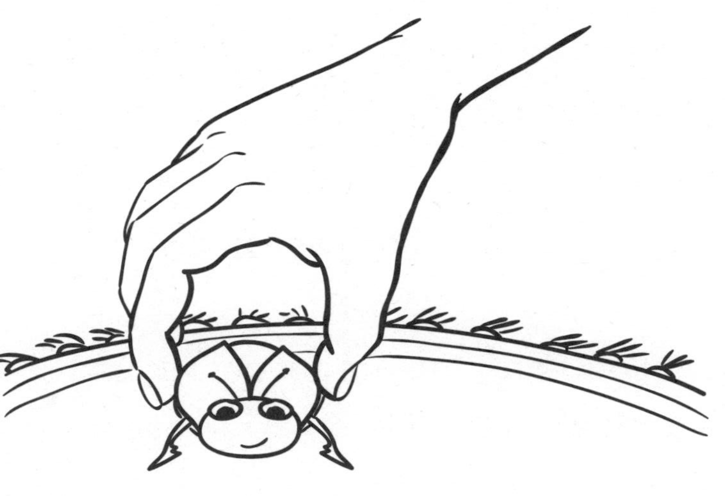

Tub, tub, tub! Lon put his dog in a tub.

Rub, rub, rub! Lon let his dog have a rub.

Hog, hog, hog! Sam has a red hog.

Bog, bog, bog! Sam and the hog went to the bog.

Top, top, top! Bob has a pot with a top.

Pop, pop, pop! The pot got hot and the top went POP!

Pit, pit, pit! Tom had a job in a pit.

Quit, quit, quit! That is the job that Tom quit.

Sun, sun, sun! Pam says, "We can run in the sun!"

Fun, fun, fun! Jen says, "Pam, you are fun!"

Name:

Ending Blends and Sight Words 2

Find the Blends

Read each word aloud. Underline the words that have an ending blend. Remember, you must be able to hear both sounds separately in an ending blend.

wish	felt	help	rush	bump
gasp	rash	melt	pulp	hatch
chomp	dish	quilt	catch	yelp
lump	tilt	quick	thump	bath

Name:

Ending Blends and Sight Words 2

By Sight

See how many sight words you can read correctly in one minute. Read aloud across the rows. When you get to the bottom, start again at the top. Keep reading until one minute has passed.

for	or	said	you	we
two	she	what	your	went
of	they	her	their	so
from	put	both	who	want
have	there	where	that	see

Number of words read correctly: ________

Sight Word Scramble

Unscramble each sight word and write it on the line provided.

1. hes ____________

2. reh ____________

3. orf ____________

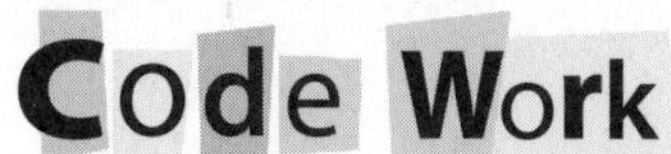

Name:

Ending Blends and Sight Words 3

Rhyme Time

Find all the words in the box that rhyme with the first word in each line below. Then write the rhyming words on the lines provided beside the first word.
Hint: You will not write a word on every line.

bank	wing	chunk	dunk	fang
hang	bonk	hung	junk	king
lung	pink	rang	bong	rung
sing	rink	tank	sunk	think
wink	yank	long	sang	thank

1. bang ________ ________ ________ ________
2. rank ________ ________ ________ ________
3. ring ________ ________ ________ ________
4. sink ________ ________ ________ ________
5. sung ________ ________ ________ ________
6. bunk ________ ________ ________ ________
7. song ________ ________ ________ ________
8. honk ________ ________ ________ ________

Name:

Ending Blends and Sight Words 3

By Sight

See how many words you can read correctly in one minute. Read aloud across the rows. When you get to the bottom of the page, start over. Try to read more words the second time.

who	for	her	of	put
said	their	want	you	or
see	they	we	your	she
two	went	so	what	both

Number of words read correctly: ________

Taft put his cot in the tent. Then the chimp, the cat, and the dog sat and had a snack. They had a chat, and then Champ, Hank, and Taft went to bed. When the sun came up, Champ gave Hank and Taft a box of milk. Then they went to have a romp in the forest. It is fun to camp!

Champ the Chimp Can Camp

Champ was a chimp. He was a chimp who had a tent. Champ put up his tent in the forest. He put his cot in the tent. Then he hung a lamp by his cot.

"Now I can camp!" Champ said.

Champ had to ask his pal, Hank, to camp with him. Hank was a cat. Champ did not want to be alone in the tent.

"I like to camp!" Hank said. "It is fun!" Hank put his cot and a rug in the tent. "I like a rug when I camp," he said, "in case the land is damp."

"What is this?" Champ said to Hank.

"It is a snack bag. Want a Zing Thing?" Hank said. The snack bag was full of Zing Things.

Then there was a crash, a bang, and a thump. It made Champ and Hank jump!

"What was that?" Champ said to Hank.

"Was it a bear?" Hank said with a gasp.

"I hope not!" Champ said.

"Let me get the lamp," Hank said.

"OK," Champ said. "I hung it by my cot."

"Who is it?" Hank said as Champ went to grasp the lamp.

"It is me, Taft!" Taft was a dog and pal. "Can I camp with you?"

"Yes, you can!" Champ said as he came out of the tent. "I am glad you want to camp with us."

Unit 6 Assessment

Part 1.

Listen to each word that is read to you. Write the blend heard at the end of each word on the lines provided.

1. ______
2. ______
3. ______
4. ______
5. ______
6. ______
7. ______
8. ______
9. ______
10. ______
11. ______
12. ______

Name:

Ending Blends and Sight Words

Part 2.

Listen to each word that is read to you. Write each word on the lines provided. Underline the blend at the end of each word.

13. __________

14. __________

15. __________

16. __________

17. __________

18. __________

19. __________

20. __________

21. __________

22. __________

Part 3.

Listen to each sentence that is read to you. Write each sentence on the lines provided.

23. ______________________________

24. ______________________________

25. ______________________________

26. ______________________________

27. ______________________________

28. ______________________________

Part 4.

In each row, underline the word that is read to you.

29.	does	for	her
30.	one	or	see
31.	she	who	why
32.	does	why	for
33.	who	her	she
34.	one	see	or
35.	why	who	she
36.	see	or	one
37.	her	for	does
38.	why	does	who
39.	for	she	her
40.	see	or	one
41.	does	see	she
42.	for	or	why
43.	her	one	who

Name:

Ending Blends and Sight Words

Part 5.

Read each word aloud.

44. why

45. does

46. for

47. who

48. she

49. her

50. one

51. see

52. or

53. for

54. she

55. her

56. does

57. why

58. one

Name:

Get Ready

Capital Letters

- **Common nouns** tell about a *general* group or kind of person, place, or thing. Common nouns are written with *lowercase* first letters. For example, *boy* and *street* are common nouns, so they are not capitalized.
- **Proper nouns** name a *particular* person, place, or thing. Proper nouns are *capitalized*. For example, *Alan* and *Riverside Road* are proper nouns, so they are capitalized.

Proper nouns include:

- Names of people and pets:

Jeff Ms. White Fluffy

- Names of streets, cities, states, and countries:

Forest Lane Mexico City Kansas England

- Names of holidays:

New Year's Day Memorial Day Labor Day

- Names of days and months:

Saturday November

- Names of buildings and bridges:

Tower of London Brooklyn Bridge

Try It

In the paragraph below, six common nouns are mistakenly capitalized. Draw a slash mark (/) through the first letters of these six common nouns to show that they should be lowercase.
Example: Boy

Also, four proper nouns are not capitalized and should be. Use the proofreading symbol (≡) to show which letters should be capitalized.
Example: jane
≡

My friend ellen and I like to walk into Town together. First we walk down Heidi Drive, then we cross the Second Street Bridge, and then we turn onto main Street. On the Fourth of july, our town is decorated with Red, White, and Blue everywhere. On saturdays, different shop owners tie colorful Balloons to lampposts. Yet, the best place to visit is the First National Bank, because they give away free Lollipops!

Name:

Beginning Blends and Sight Words 1

Choose the Blend

Underline the blend that completes the word. Write the word on the line provided.

Example: ______ ush bl gl cl blush

1. ______ an sl pl gl ____________
2. ______ ap gl fl bl ____________
3. ______ ock sl pl cl ____________
4. ______ ad bl gl fl ____________
5. ______ ed sl gl cl ____________
6. ______ ack pl bl gl ____________
7. ______ ug pl cl bl ____________
8. ______ ap gl bl sl ____________
9. ______ ock sl bl pl ____________
10. ______ am bl cl pl ____________
11. ______ ob gl fl cl ____________
12. ______ ag bl pl fl ____________

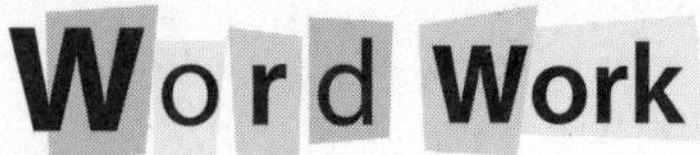

Name:

Beginning Blends and Sight Words 1

Sentences

Choose the words from the box that best complete each sentence below. Write each word on the lines provided.

does	why	one

1. I wonder ____________ he is so sad.

2. I have ____________ dollar in my pocket.

3. My mom ____________ not like candy.

Sight Work

Underline the sight word listed as many times as it appears in each row. An example has been done for you.

Example: and <u>and</u> as <u>and</u> an an

4. why	who	what	why	they	why
5. she	he	she	see	she	her
6. for	of	for	or	or	of
7. does	says	was	does	was	does
8. one	one	on	on	one	one
9. her	her	he	her	she	her

Name:

Beginning Blends and Sight Words 2

Choose the Blend

Underline the blend that completes the word given. Then, write the word on the line provided. Say each word aloud when done. An example has been done for you.

Example:	pr	fr	br	____ ag	brag
1.	fr	cr	tr	____ og	__________
2.	pr	gr	tr	____ ab	__________
3.	cr	pr	br	____ int	__________
4.	dr	fr	cr	____ ash	__________
5.	dr	fr	pr	____ um	__________
6.	tr	pr	gr	____ ash	__________
7.	fr	dr	cr	____ ib	__________
8.	pr	gr	dr	____ and	__________
9.	fr	tr	br	____ ip	__________
10.	gr	cr	fr	____ ame	__________
11.	pr	tr	gr	____ une	__________
12.	tr	fr	dr	____ ag	__________
13.	br	dr	gr	____ ick	__________

Sight Word Practice

Read aloud each sight word in the box below.

we	does	my
for	are	why
she	one	her

Find and underline each sight word given above in the jumble below.
Hint: There is one sight word in each row of letters.

e	a	r	e
d	o	e	s
s	h	e	s
i	d	w	e
f	h	e	r
m	y	v	o
u	w	h	y
o	n	e	z
t	f	o	r

Find the Word

Read each sentence. Find the word that begins with the beginning blend *shr* or *thr*. Write the word on the line. Then say the word aloud.

1. See the nest in the shrub.

   ____

2. Thrift means to save cash.

   ____

3. Socks can shrink in the wash.

   ____

4. We watch the thrush.

   ____

5. The dog thrust his nose in the dish.

   ____

6. Mom and Dad like shrimp for lunch.

   ____

7. Tom felt a throb in his hand.

   ____

8. That bad cat shred the cloth!

   ____

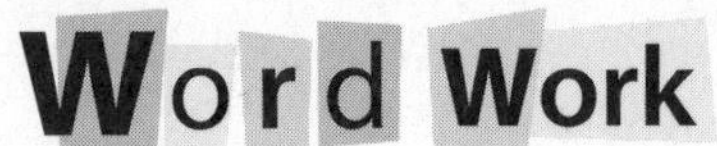

Name:

Beginning Blends and Sight Words 3

Sight Word Search

Read the sight words in the box below. Find each word in the word search and circle it.

does	were	why	my	are	one

y	d	o	e	s	t	e	w	i
i	s	w	e	a	r	e	y	o
m	y	e	d	m	o	e	p	n
o	s	r	w	h	y	t	u	e
d	l	e	d	s	t	y	r	e
y	o	o	d	g	t	e	w	e

Sentences

Choose the words from the box that best complete each sentence. Write the words on the lines provided.

my	were	are

1. We ______________ all sick on Monday.
2. Today is ______________ birthday.
3. You ______________ going home now.

"Yes," said Brad, "I am glad that you had a yen for shrimp. This is a fine lunch."

Just when Brad went to take a bite, a thrush came by to grab his shrimp.

"Stop!" Brad said to the thrush. "That is my shrimp! Get back!" But the shrimp was lost to the thrush. The thrush sat on a shrub by the bench and ate the shrimp in a big gulp. Trent had to chuckle.

"Lucky you got two of those!" he said to Brad. "One box of shrimp for you, and one box of shrimp for the thrush!"

The Shrimp Shack

Trent and Brad were on the job. Trent went up to Brad, who was at his desk.

"What is for lunch?" Trent said to Brad.

"I am not sure," Brad said with a shrug. "What can we have?"

"Shrimp!" Trent said. "I have a yen for shrimp."

"Then shrimp it is!" Brad said. "Where can we get it?"

"At The Shrimp Shack," Trent said. "It

is on Shred Lane by the Thrift Shop," Trent said.

The two men got up and went to get lunch. It was a short hop to The Shrimp Shack.

"What can I get you?" the clerk said to Trent.

"I want a big shrimp box," Trent said. "And a can of pop."

"I want the same," Brad said. "Make that two! But I want a malt, not a can of pop."

"OK," said the clerk. "I can get that for you in a flash."

The clerk gave Brad and Trent a big sack. They gave the clerk cash and went to sit on a bench in the warm sun.

"I like this shrimp," Trent said as he had a bite.

Blend Scramble

Unscramble the letters to make a word. Write the word on the line provided.
Hint: Each word begins with a blend.

Example: wgis   swig

1. psit ______________
2. wipse ______________
3. shast ______________
4. kisp ______________
5. anps ______________
6. msgo ______________
7. canks ______________
8. tosp ______________
9. tasdn ______________
10. mwis ______________
11. dkis ______________
12. nacs ______________
13. ekoms ______________
14. sacb ______________

Sight Word Sentences

Choose the word from the box that best completes each sentence. Write the words on the lines provided.

were	my	Dr.	are	Mr.	Mrs.

1. My mom is called __________ Smith.
2. My shoes __________ too tight.
3. My dad is called __________ Smith.
4. Tom and Joe __________ gone yesterday.
5. We went to see __________ Sam when I hurt my leg.
6. He took __________ coat.

Name:

Beginning Blends and Sight Words 4

Get Ready

Singular and Plural Possessive Nouns

If you possess something, you own it. **Possessive nouns** show *ownership*.

A **singular** possessive noun shows that *one* person, place, thing, or idea has ownership.

Fred's dog	the dog owned by Fred
a day's work	the work of one day

A **plural** possessive noun shows that *more than one* person, place, thing, or idea has ownership.

the Chens' party	the party that the Chen family had
kids' fingerprints	the fingerprints made by many kids

Singular Possessive Nouns

To form the singular possessive, add an apostrophe and an *–s* to the singular noun.

Singular	Singular Possessive
Tom	Tom's notebook
cat	cat's paw

Plural Possessive Nouns

To form a plural possessive noun, usually you just add an apostrophe to the end of the plural noun. You can use this rule for any plural noun that ends in *–s*.

Singular	Plural	Plural Possessive
pig	pigs	pigs' pens
fox	foxes	foxes' tails

Try It

Read each word. Write the singular possessive, the plural form, and the plural possessive for each word on the lines provided.

	Singular Noun	Singular Possessive	Plural Noun	Plural Possessive
Example:	cub	cub's	cubs	cubs'
	dish			
	pit			
	kite			
	box			
	bunch			
	nest			
	fact			
	truth			

Name:

Beginning Blends

Draw a line from the words in the first column to the words in the second column that contain the same beginning blend.

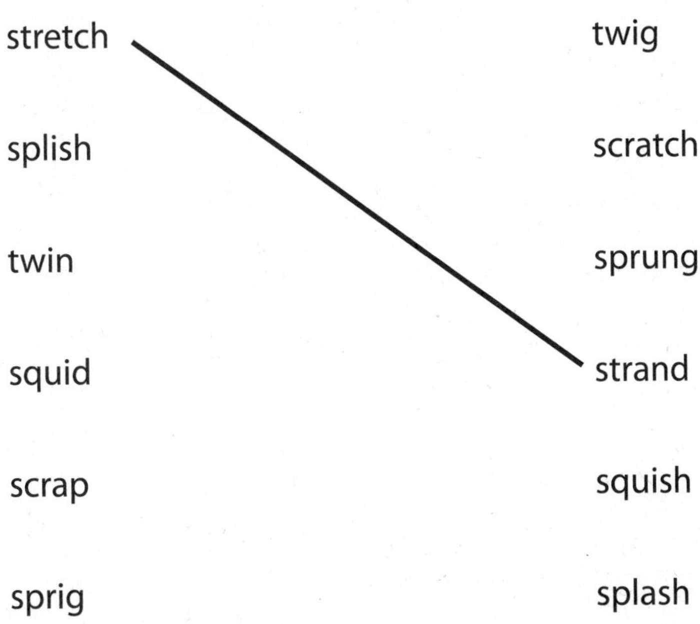

In each sentence, underline the word that has a beginning blend. Then write the word on the line provided.

1. Tim ran up the path in a sprint. ____________
2. The bug went splat on the rug. ____________
3. Jake can bend and stretch. ____________
4. That dog has a twitch. ____________
5. "Scram!" the man said to the kid. ____________
6. The cat can squash the tick. ____________

Sight Word Sentences

Choose the abbreviations from the box that best complete each sentence. Write each abbreviation on the lines provided.

Mr.	Mrs.	Dr.

1. I have to go see ________ May for a checkup.
2. ________ Jones gave me five dollars to mow his lawn.
3. It was cold so ________ Smith wore her coat.

Sight Word Recognition

Underline the sight word listed as many times as it appears in each row. An example has been done for you.

Example: on <u>on</u> in <u>on</u> is in

4.	Mr.	Mrs.	Dr.	Mr.	Mrs.	Mr.
5.	were	were	where	were	where	were
6.	Dr.	Mr.	Mr.	Dr.	Mr.	Dr.
7.	Mrs.	Mr.	Mr.	Mrs.	Dr.	Mrs.
8.	my	my	why	my	why	my
9.	are	and	or	are	and	Are

Twig. "What do you think it is?" she asks. Mr. Twig thinks. Then Mrs. Twig says, "Oh, no! It's the soap!" "The soap?" asks Dr. Strand. "It must be the soap we had for the bath! The shop did not have my brand of soap. So I got a soap that was on sale." "Yes, that must be it!" says Dr. Strand. "That brand of soap must be bad for Max and his skin." Mrs. Twig gives Max a hug.

"I am so sorry, Max," she says. Dr. Strand tells Mr. and Mrs. Twig that it is not bad to fix. She gives them the name of a gel they can use to make the itch go away. Mrs. Twig jots the name in a note pad. "Thanks, Dr. Strand," Mr. Twig says. When they get the gel, Mrs. Twig rubs it all over Max. Max stops to scratch in a snap! Max starts to yap. He says, "Thanks, Dr. Strand! You are the best!"

Max Takes a Bath

Splish splash! Time for a bath for Max! Max is a big, black dog. He has so much mud on his fur! Mr. Twig takes Max out back. He helps Max get into the tub. Mrs. Twig gets Max wet with the hose. Max likes to get wet. Mr. Twig takes the soap and rubs it all over Max. Max likes his bath. He pokes the bubbles with his nose. Pop! Gus, the cat, comes to sit and watch Max get his bath. Gus is not like Max. He does not like to get wet. Mrs. Twig gives Gus a quick spray with the

hose as a joke. "Scram, Gus!" Mrs. Twig says to the cat. Gus jumps up. He runs and hides. Mrs. Twig begins to smile. See you later, Gus!

Now it is time for the last part of the bath. Mrs. Twig sprays him to get rid of the soap. Then Mr. Twig claps his hands. Max jumps out of the tub. Mr. and Mrs.

Twig stand back. Max has to twist and twitch. He has to shake out his fur. He sprays Mr. and Mrs. Twig. They get wet. Then Mrs. Twig pats Max with a twill rag. "Max has no mud on his fur!" Mrs. Twig says. "I am so glad we gave Max a bath."

The next day, Max has an itch. He has to scratch. He has to scratch his leg. He has to scratch his nose. Max cannot stop. He has to scratch and scratch! "We need to take Max to the vet," says Mrs. Twig. "I bet she can say what will help Max." Mr. Twig puts Max in the van. Then they drive to see Dr. Strand.

"It is his skin," says Dr. Strand. "What makes his skin itch? He has to scratch the itch!" Mr. Twig thinks. Mrs. Twig thinks.

"What do you think it is?" Mr. Twig asks Mrs. Twig. "I can not say," says Mrs.

Name:

Unit 7 Assessment

Part 1.

Listen to each word that is read to you. Write each word on the lines provided.

1. ____________
2. ____________
3. ____________
4. ____________
5. ____________
6. ____________
7. ____________
8. ____________
9. ____________
10. ____________

Assessment

Name:

Beginning Blends and Sight Words

Part 2.

Read each sentence. Underline the word that best completes each sentence.

11. "I want some milk, ______," said Tom. (too, two)

12. Grant has a ______ cat. (brick, black)

13. Trent broke the ______ to his backpack. (strap, scrap)

14. I am ______ that you won the game! (glad, grand)

15. Sam put the ______ in the bin. (twist, trash)

Part 3.

Listen to each word that is read to you. Underline the beginning blend that is contained in each word.

16. sk sl sm sp spr st str

17. sl sm sn sp squ st sw

18. sk sl sp spr squ st str

19. sl sm sn sp st str sw

20. sc sl sp spr squ st str

Name:

Beginning Blends and Sight Words

Part 4.

Listen to each word that is read to you. Write each word on the lines provided.

21. ____________

22. ____________

23. ____________

24. ____________

25. ____________

26. ____________

27. ____________

28. ____________

29. ____________

30. ____________

Part 5.

In each row, underline the word that is read to you.

31.	split	sprint	spit
32.	wink	work	walk
33.	flash	fresh	flesh
34.	prim	plan	print
35.	stung	smug	slug
36.	splat	spat	slap
37.	take	talk	tack
38.	twin	tin	trim
39.	Mrs.	Dr.	Mr.
40.	skimp	stamp	strand
41.	stash	slash	squash
42.	you	too	who
43.	fog	frog	flog
44.	one	win	on
45.	sled	shed	shred

Name:

Beginning Blends and Sight Words 6

Get Ready

- Verbs in sentences tell what the subject does or is. **Action verbs** tell what the subject *does*. Read the following sentences with action verbs:

    Andrew *eats* pizza for supper every Tuesday.

    The cheetah *ran* across the plain.

    Squirrels *climb* to the tops of trees.

    I *remember* that book very well.

Sometimes the action of a verb is *physical* and easy to see.

hit, dig, drag, kick

Sometimes the action of a verb is *mental* (in your head) and not as easy to see.

think, like, hope, enjoy

Being verbs tell what someone or something *is or is like*. It makes a connection between the subject and other words that tell more about the subject.

That motorcycle was very fast.

subject = *motorcycle*

being verb = *was*

more about the subject = *very fast*

Being verbs are different forms of the verb *to be*. Study the list of common being verbs below.

is	was	am	has been	have been
are	were	be	had been	will be

Name:

Try It

Choose the *action verb* from the box below that best completes each sentence. Write each verb on the lines provided.

dug	like	shut	think

1. Jan and Dan __________ to watch TV.
2. Tom __________ a hole in the dirt.
3. Gus __________ the lid to the box.
4. Do you __________ you can help me wash my car?

Choose the *being verb* from the box below that best completes each sentence. Write each verb on the lines provided.

is	were	be	was

5. Mark __________ my best pal.
6. That game __________ fun!
7. Can you __________ at the park by six o'clock?
8. Pat and Mike __________ too late to catch the bus.

Double Trouble Endings

Underline the double letter ending in each word. Then say the words aloud and write each word on the lines provided.

Example: shell shell

1. fuzz ______
2. grass ______
3. stuff ______
4. well ______
5. pass ______
6. sniff ______
7. brass ______
8. buzz ______
9. spill ______
10. mess ______
11. chill ______

Sight Word Recognition

Underline the sight word listed as many times as it appears in each row. An example has been done for you.

Example:	and	and	as	and	an	an
1.	too	who	talk	too	they	too
2.	Dr.	Mr.	Dr.	Mr.	Dr.	Mrs.
3.	walk	what	walk	talk	what	talk
4.	Mr.	Mr.	Mrs.	Mr.	Mrs.	Mr.
5.	Mrs.	Mrs.	Dr.	Mr.	Mrs.	Mrs.
6.	talk	talk	walk	talk	walk	talk

Sight Word Sentences

Choose the words from the box that best complete each sentence. Write the words on the lines provided.

too	walk	talk

7. I like to take the dog for a ________.

8. This hat is ________ big.

9. I will ________ to Bob.

snake pass. We all go back to playing on the grass in the park.

Later on, the sun begins to set. It gets dark fast. There is a chill in the air. I call to Nell. "Come here, Nell!" She runs over to Jeff and me. Then I call for Jess. "Here, boy!" He runs over to us, too. We all put on our jackets. It is time to walk home.

When we get home, we talk with Mom. She went to a store at the mall where they sell fun things. She got a brass bell for Jill, her boss. Jill has a ship. Mom lets us ring the bell. Ding! Ding! Ding!

Just then Dad comes home. Mom tells us to wash up for dinner. We tell Mom and Dad what we did at the park. It was a good day!

Fun on the Grass

Mom calls all us kids to come over by her. She tells us that Dad is gone. He had to play at a show with his jazz band. And Mom has to shop at the mall. She wants to drop us off at the park. So, we all pile in the car. Mom tells us to come home when the sun sets. We tell her we will. "Have a fun time!" she yells as she drives off.

I like the park. There is so much to do! Jeff kicks a ball across the grass. I run to get it. I trip over a rock and fall. I cut my leg.

I bet I will get a scab. Oh, well! I get up and kick the ball back to Jeff. We pass the ball back and forth. I never miss. I like to kick the ball!

Nell sits on a blanket and plays with her doll. Nell takes a sip of soda pop. She likes the fizz! Nell gets up and spills the

soda pop on her dress. What a mess! I help Nell mop up the soda pop. No fuss, no muss! Nell says, "Thank you!" She gives me a kiss.

Over by a brick wall, Jess, the dog, finds a tall plant. The top of the plant has pods that look like fuzz balls. It is called a milkweed. Jess gives it a sniff with his nose. Nell walks over and picks a pod from the plant. She gives the pod a puff. The silk of the milkweed takes off!

Now we hear a bell chime. It comes from the big clock on the hill. The hands of the clock tell us it is time for lunch. We all sit on the blanket. I fill a glass with soda pop. We munch our lunch. I have a dill pickle. Yum!

Jeff stands up. He hears a hiss in the grass. It is a snake! We tell Nell it will not hurt her. It is a kind snake. We let the

Name:

More Than One

Read the base words in the first column. Some take the ending, –*s*, when becoming plural. Others take the ending, –*es*. Decide which plural ending each base word takes. Then write the new words on the lines provided.
Hint: Base words ending in *s*, *sh*, *ch*, *x*, or *z* take the –*es* ending.

Base Word	**Base Word + Plural Ending**
Example: box	boxes
1. cat	__________
2. nut	__________
3. dish	__________
4. buzz	__________
5. watch	__________
6. bat	__________
7. dress	__________
8. hip	__________
9. glass	__________
10. bus	__________
11. snack	__________

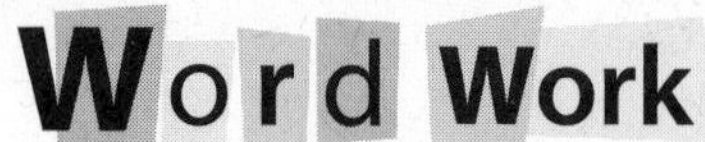

Name:

Word Endings and Sight Words 2

Sight Words Scramble

Unscramble each sight word and write it on the line provided.

1. lupl ______________
2. oto ______________
3. uto ______________
4. lakw ______________
5. aaing ______________
6. klat ______________

Which Word?

Choose the words from the box that best complete each sentence. Write the words on the lines provided.

again	out	pull

7. Can we do that ______________?
8. Do not ______________ on that string.
9. I will take the dog ______________.

Ending *–ed*

Read the rule above each table. Add the ending *–ed* to each base word in the table by following the rule given. Write the new word in the second column. Then say the sound the ending *–ed* makes in that word.

Rule: Double the single ending consonant of a one-syllable word. Then add *–ed*.

Base Word	Base Word with Ending *–ed*
nod	nodded
pat	
pop	
plan	

Rule: Drop the silent *e*, then add *–ed*.

Base Word	Base Word with Ending *–ed*
rake	
fade	
hope	
pile	

Rule: Don't change anything; just add *–ed*.

Base Word	Base Word with Ending *–ed*
land	
last	
rush	
walk	

Name:

Word Endings and Sight Words 3

Sight Words Scramble and Sentence Completion

Unscramble each sight word. Use each word to complete the sentences below. Read each sentence aloud. Then write a new sentence using each sight word.

ulpl ____________

tou ____________

naiag ____________

1. Can you ____________ the truck with a rope?
2. I want to hike the hill ____________ .
3. Tom went ____________ to go for a walk.

4. ____

____

5. ____

____

6. ____

____

"OK, I'll get back on the path," Ling said as she hopped off the rock. "But that was fun to find a bat!" Ling was thrilled. She hugged Ted. "I am glad you looked up at it!" Ted smiled and nodded.

"It was no big thing," Ted said as he kicked a small rock. He was just glad that Ling was not mad at him any more!

The Hike

Ted and Ling went for a hike in the forest in the spring. They walked and walked. They stopped when they spotted a nest filled with eggs. They stopped again when an elk jumped across the path. They stopped one more time when they glimpsed moss that looked like string. Ted picked up the moss. Then he sniffed it. He said it smelled like rust! He handed the clump of moss to Ling. Ling looked at it, then she dumped the moss back on a rock.

Ted and Ling set out on their walk again. But then Ted left the path and got lost.

"Ted, where are you?" Ling yelled. "Ted!" she called out.

"Here I am!" Ted yelled back. He jumped out of a bunch of bushes. "I went off the path. I was lost for a second."

"I told you not to step off the path," Ling said as she pulled him next to her. She was mad. "You are lucky I stopped to look for you!"

"I just was not watching what I was doing," Ted said. "I hope I did not make you mad." Ling did not look at him. She just kept walking. This time Ted was sure to walk next to Ling. But then he fell back again.

"Pick it up!" she said. "I am not walking that fast, and I need to get home."

Ted rushed to catch up to Ling. Then he stopped in his tracks.

"What is that?" Ted asked.

"What are you talking about?" Ling asked.

"There!" Ted yelled. "The black thing that is hanging off that branch." Ling looked up.

"Gosh!" she said. "That is one big bat!" Ling stepped up on a rock to get a better look.

"What are you doing, Ling?" Ted quizzed. "Get back from that pest!" Ted did not like her standing next to a bat. He said it was not safe.

Unit 8 Assessment

Part 1.

Read each word below. Then say it aloud. Decide which sound *–ed* makes at the end of the word. Underline the sound you hear.

1.	landed	/ed/	/d/	/t/
2.	fussed	/ed/	/d/	/t/
3.	filled	/ed/	/d/	/t/
4.	watched	/ed/	/d/	/t/
5.	boxed	/ed/	/d/	/t/
6.	kissed	/ed/	/d/	/t/
7.	grunted	/ed/	/d/	/t/
8.	buzzed	/ed/	/d/	/t/
9.	spotted	/ed/	/d/	/t/
10.	grabbed	/ed/	/d/	/t/

Name:

Word Endings and Sight Words

Part 2.

Listen to each word that is read to you. Write each word on the lines provided.

11. ______________________

12. ______________________

13. ______________________

14. ______________________

15. ______________________

16. ______________________

17. ______________________

18. ______________________

19. ______________________

20. ______________________

☼ Assessment

Name:

Word Endings and Sight Words

Part 3.

Listen to each sentence that is read to you. Write each sentence on the lines provided.

21. ______________________________

22. ______________________________

23. ______________________________

24. ______________________________

25. ______________________________

Part 4.

Read each word and name aloud.

26. again

27. out

28. pull

29. Dr. Tell

30. friend

31. Mrs. Siff

32. out

33. too

34. next

35. Mr. Russ

Name:

Word Endings and Sight Words

Part 5.

In each row, underline the word that is read to you.

36.	toe	too	do
37.	pull	put	see
38.	we	my	me
39.	pen	end	again
40.	talk	tan	tuck
41.	or	out	at
42.	next	net	nest
43.	find	end	friend
44.	want	walk	watch
45.	ask	again	are

Part 6.

Read each name aloud.

46. Dr. Will

47. Mrs. Friend

48. Mr. Cliff

49. Dr. Buzz

50. Mrs. Liss

Word Endings and Sight Words 4

Get Ready

- Many verbs need more than one word to express their meaning. For example:

  Jan *is going* to the shop.

  She *will get* a new dress.

- This kind of verb has two parts: a **main verb** and a **helping verb**. The helping verb does exactly what the name says. It helps the main verb.

  I am chatting with my friend.

  Helping verb: *am*

  Main verb: *chatting*

- Main verbs can have more than one helping verb.

  We *have been sitting* in the bus for a long time.

  Helping verbs: *have been*

  Main verb: *sitting*

- Study the list of helping verbs below:

am	was	has	will	is
were	have	can	are	been
had	might	be		

Name:

Try It

In the sentences below, write **M** over the main verb and **H** over the helping verb or verbs. Remember that a main verb can have more than one helping verb.

1. The fox is hiding in the grass.

2. We have been watching the foxes all day.

3. I will talk to my friends about foxes.

Name:

The Sound /f/

Read each sentence aloud. Find the word in each sentence that contains the sound /f/. Write that word on the line provided. Read the sentence again.
Hint: One sentence contains more than one word with the sound /f/.

1. Pick up the phone. ____________
2. Ralph made a graph. ____________
3. Steph threw the ball. ____________
4. Phil smiled at the joke. ____________
5. The dolphin swam and jumped. ____________

Write three sentences. In each sentence, use one word with the sound /f/ spelled with *ph*.

6. ____________________________
7. ____________________________
8. ____________________________

Name:

Sight Words Scramble

Unscramble each sight word and write it on the line provided.

1. fdnier ____________
2. naiag ____________
3. ualhg ____________
4. tou ____________
5. xent ____________
6. lulp ____________

Sentences

Choose the words from the box that best complete each sentence. Write each word on the lines provided.

next	laugh	friend

7. I will have some ____________ time.
8. I had to ____________ at the chimp!
9. My ____________ went with me to the game.

It's in my bag." Kat got the small gizmo out of the bag. She handed it to Pat. Pat turned it on and punched a tab or two.

"Turn left at the next stop," a man's voice said. The voice came out of the gizmo.

"Oh, my!" Kat laughed. "This thing is talking to us! It can tell where we are! It's like magic!" The two old gals smiled at each other. "OK, let's get moving!" Kat said to Pat. "It will be getting dark in a bit. I need to get home and make dinner!"

"OK!" said Pat as she stepped on the gas. She turned left at the next stop, just like the voice told her. She did what the voice told her, too, until they were home. It really was like magic!

Where Are We?

It was such a fine day. Pat said to herself, "I think I will take a drive!" Pat phoned her best friend, Kat. Pat and Kat were longtime friends. Pat asked Kat if she wanted to go for a ride in her big car. Kat was thrilled! Pat got in her car and picked up Kat at her home. Then she drove the two of them out to the sticks. In a bit, Pat pulled over. Then she took off the top of her car and put it in the trunk. "Oh, this is swell!" Kat said to

Pat. "Now I can smell the fresh grass! I like this car!" Pat took a scarf from her bag and handed it to Kat.

"Use this to keep your locks from getting messed up," Pat said as she put

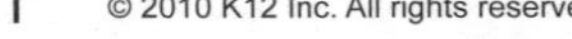

one on, too. "How is your son, Ralph?" Pat asked Kat as she started up the car again. "Did he have fun on his trip to Rome?" Pat got on the path and drove on.

"Oh, yes, he did!" Kat said. "He even got to meet a king while he was there." Kat told Pat all about her son's trip. The two gals saw many things while they drove and talked, like a pack of wild dogs, a thrush on a log, and a big lake.

"I think it's time to go back home now," Pat said at 4:00.

"Where are we?" Kat asked Pat.

"I can't tell!" Pat said to Kat. They didn't know what to do. They were far from home by now. "Just a moment! I have this new gizmo. It's called a GPS," said Pat. "My son, Phil, just gave it to me.

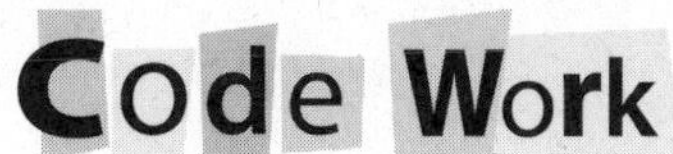

Name:

Words with Soft *c* and Soft *g*

Write each word with a soft *c*, as in *ace*, in the box below.
Hint: Seven words have a soft *c*.

twice catch
call cinch
came place
nice cash
camp cell
chance since

words with a soft *c*

Write each word with a soft *g*, as in *age*, in the box below.
Hint: Seven words have a soft *g*.

hinge huge
gym goes
bulge gem
hug gust
page stage
begin twig

words with a soft *g*

Sight Word Sentences

Choose the words from the box that best complete each sentence. Write the words on the lines provided.

anything	goes	begin
next	laugh	friend

1. Please do not ________________ at me.
2. ________________ would be better than this.
3. I am ________________ in line.
4. Soon the show will ________________ .
5. Henry ________________ to the store every day.
6. My ________________ Sam is sick today.

Complete the sentence below by using three words from the box above. Write the words on the lines provided.

My ________________ Arnold will ________________ at ________________ .

r-Controlled Vowels

Underline each word in the box that contains the sound /er/, as in *her*.

brush	squirm	shirt	term	trim
stir	fist	first	shrimp	stern
thrill	swirl	third	thirst	trip
trust	verb	gem	germs	twirl

Your Turn!

On the lines provided, write two words that contain the sound /er/ spelled *er*. (Choose words *not* shown in the box above.)

1. ______________________

2. ______________________

On the lines provided, write two words that contain the sound /er/ spelled *ir*. (Choose words *not* shown in the box above.)

3. ______________________

4. ______________________

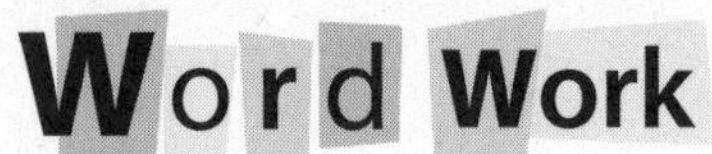

Name:

Difficult Spellings & r-Controlled Vowels and Sight Words 3

Sight Words Scramble

Unscramble each sight word. Write each unscrambled word on the lines provided. Then use each word to complete the sentences below.

ganniyht ________________

eibgn ________________

sgeo ________________

1. The movie will ________________ in five minutes.
2. I cannot hear ________________ when I wear my earplugs.
3. My family ________________ to the beach every summer.

Sentences

On the lines provided, write a sentence for each sight word unscrambled above.

4. ____

____

5. ____

____

6. ____

____

into the churning and whirling water. Burl grabbed his surfboard and he swam back to where Tucker was sitting on her board watching him. He pulled himself out of the water and sat next to her.

"You did well for your first crack at it," she said. "You got to the end of your surfboard before you fell off. Nice!" Another big wave came by. The two jumped up on their boards. Tucker was just standing up when a she heard a bird chirp. It landed on her surfboard! "This blackbird wants to hang ten!" Tucker yelled to Burl. "Watch!" The bird hopped to the end of her surfboard and perched on the tip. Tucker kept back so as not to disturb the bird.

"A bird that can hang ten!" Burl said. "That bird puts me to shame!"

Surf's Up!

Burl likes to surf. He goes surfing as much as he can. Burl says the best place to surf is west of the cliffs at Blackbird Bluff. There are big waves there. Burl likes to surf the big waves the best!

Burl met his friend, Tucker, on the sand by the big rock. Tucker is a girl. She likes to surf just as much as Burl does. They tossed their surfboards in the water and paddled out to the big waves.

They were in luck! The first wave that came up was perfect. They both jumped on their boards to begin surfing. Tucker made a turn on the face of the wave and got in front of Burl.

"Watch this trick I just learned!" Tucker yelled to Burl. He watched as Tucker edged up her surfboard until she was perched on the tip.

"What are you doing?" Burl yelled to Tucker.

"This is called *hanging ten*," Tucker yelled back to him. "All ten of my toes are hanging off the edge of my surfboard!" Tucker jumped off her board, and then Burl did the same. They paddled back out and sat on their surfboards to rest for a bit.

"Wow!" Burl said to Tucker. "That was a clever stunt!" She flashed a smile at him.

"Check out that big wave," Tucker said. "Your turn!" she giggled. Burl got up on his surfboard. He made it to the tip. Then, SPLASH! Burl fell off his board and

Name:

r-Controlled Vowels

Sort the words in the box according to their spelling of the sound /er/. Write each word in the correct column.

after	burn	clerk	curb
fern	girl	heard	herd
learn	stir	third	thirst
yearn	earth	hurt	turn

er	*ir*	*ur*	*ear*

Choose the words from the box above that best complete each sentence below. Write each word on the lines provided. Then read each sentence aloud.

1. I would like to ____________ to play baseball.
2. The ____________ helped her brother fix his bike.
3. Please ____________ the soup so it does not ____________.
4. I ____________ the duck quack as it swam in the pond.
5. The ____________ of sheep moved together in the field.

Complete the Sentences

Use the sight words from the box to complete each sentence below. **Hint:** One word will be used in two sentences. Then read each sentence aloud.

after	begin	down	goes	know	anything

1. Pat ______________ camping every summer.
2. Do you ______________ how to play chess?
3. I went to bed ______________ I brushed my teeth.
4. The cat did not want to climb ______________ from the tree.
5. Eve played with her friends ______________ she cleaned her room.
6. Can I help you with ______________ to get ready for the party?
7. We will ______________ planting the garden on Saturday morning.

Difficult Spellings & r-Controlled Vowels and Sight Words 4

Get Ready

- The *regular* ending for **past** and **past participle verbs** is –*d* or –*ed*. Some verbs are irregular and don't follow the usual rules. Past and past participle forms of *irregular* verbs do *not* end in –*d* or –*ed*.

- Irregular verbs are unpredictable, so you must practice and learn them. Study the list of some irregular verbs below. Pick any three verbs from the list and make up sentences with the present, past, and past participle. For example, for *eat*:

  I *eat* my peas with honey.

  I *ate* peas with my marshmallow sandwich.

  I *have eaten* too many peas and marshmallows.

Present	**Past**	**Past Participle**
bring	brought	(has) brought
buy	bought	(have) bought
come	came	(has) come
cut	cut	(have) cut
do	did	(has) done
eat	ate	(have) eaten
feel	felt	(has) felt
give	gave	(have) given
go	went	(has) gone
is (am, are)	was (were)	(have) been
know	knew	(has) known
make	made	(have) made
run	ran	(has) run
see	saw	(have) seen
sit	sat	(has) sat
understand	understood	(have) understood
take	took	(has) taken
tear	tore	(have) torn

Name:

Try It

Write the missing forms of each word on the lines provided.

	Present	Past	Past Participle
1.	drip	dripped	(has) ______
2.	know	______	(have) ______
3.	______	cut	(has) ______
4.	cry	______	(have) cried
5.	give	______	(has) given
6.	______	went	(have) ______

Choose one verb from above and write sentences using the present, past, and past participle forms of that verb. Then read your sentences aloud.

7. Present: ______________________________

____

8. Past: ______________________________

____

9. Past participle: ______________________________

____

Name:

/ar/ and /or/

Choose the word from the box that best completes each sentence. Write each word on the lines provided. Then underline the letters that make the sound /ar/, as in *car*, or the sound /or/, as in *horn*, in each word.

art	force	fork	March
Mark	scarf	sports	thorn

1. You use a __________ to eat.
2. __________ is a boy's name.
3. __________ is the month before April.
4. The stem of that rose has a sharp __________ .
5. Do you have a __________ to keep your neck warm?
6. Painting and pottery are two kinds of __________ .
7. Baseball and basketball are two kinds of __________ .
8. If you make others do something, you __________ them.

Sight Words Scramble and Sentences

Unscramble each sight word. Write each word on the lines provided.

1. aefrt ____________
2. dnow ____________
3. aghinnty ____________
4. eogs ____________
5. eibgn ____________
6. oknw ____________

On the lines provided below, write each sight word from above in a sentence. Then read each sentence aloud.

7. ______________________________

8. ______________________________

9. ______________________________

10. ______________________________

11. ______________________________

12. ______________________________

clerk in the candle shop came running outside. The girl was in shock, but she wasn't burned.

Mark held his hurt arm as he stared at the mess. It was a disaster! No wonder his mother told him not to play with his ball in the front yard! What a lesson Mark learned that day.

The firemen got there before you could blink an eye. They put out the fire in no time. The only person who was hurt was Mark. He had a torn shirt and a sore arm. All Mark could think about was all the money he was going to have to earn to pay for all the damage. It took a long time before the car, the van, and the store were repaired. You can be sure of one thing: Mark never kicked the ball in the front yard again!

Mind Your Mother

Mark is thirteen. He likes to play kickball. He likes to kick the ball hard. But his mother made a rule. She told Mark he may only kick his ball in the backyard. Mark didn't know why his mother made this rule. What is the harm in playing kickball in the front yard with the other kids? But Mark was a good boy, and he did what his mother said.

One afternoon, Bert came over to play with Mark. Bert wanted to play kickball in Mark's front yard. "You know that is against the rules," Mark said to Bert. But Mark's mother was at the store. Mark figured she would never know. So, Mark and Bert started to kick the ball back and forth in the front yard. It was fun. They were having a wonderful time. Then Mark kicked the ball so hard Bert missed it. The ball hit the fir tree at the end of the yard. Then the ball rolled into the street. Mark started to run after it. Oh, no! A car was coming! The car was about to hit the ball and Mark. The man in the car honked the horn. It startled Mark. Mark fell down hard on his arm. The car had to swerve. BANG! The car crashed into a purple van that was parked on the side of the street.

The van lurched forward. It hit a fire plug. WHOOSH! The fire plug fell over. Water began to squirt into the air. Just

then, the driver jumped out of the van. But the van didn't stop moving! It started to roll down the hill. There is a curve at the bottom of the hill. When the van got to the curve, it jumped the curb. CRASH! It smashed into the window of the candle shop. Glass showered down. For a moment, it was very quiet. Then, KA-POW! The van burst into flames! The

Name:

Difficult Spellings & r-Controlled Vowels and Sight Words 6

Complete the Sentence

Read each word in the box aloud. Choose the word from the box that best completes each sentence. Write each word on the lines provided. Then read each sentence aloud.
Hint: One word is used twice.

bread	breath	dealt	head	meant	thread

1. I can ________________ the needle.
2. Mom ________________ what she said.
3. I like peanut butter on my ________________ .
4. This ________________ is perfect for my shirt.
5. He ________________ the cards so we could play the game.
6. Dad stopped to catch his ________________ during our jog.
7. She was careful not to hit her ________________ as she got into the car.

By Sight

See how many words you can read correctly in one minute. Read aloud across the rows. When you get to the bottom of the page, start over. Try to read more words the second time.

Dr.	mother	does	only	down
next	pull	goes	begin	know
talk	friend	Mrs.	again	anything
too	walk	my	after	Mr.
out	were	are	my	father

Number of words read correctly: ______

Get Ready

- Verbs in English have four principal forms:

1. Present
2. Present participle (uses helping verbs *is, am, are, was, were*)
3. Past
4. Past participle (uses helping verbs *has, have, had*)

You form the past and past participle of a regular verb by adding *–d* or *–ed*. For example, *walk* becomes *walked*. However, you just have to learn the past and past participle forms of irregular verbs because—well, because they're not regular!

- Study the principal forms of the following *irregular* verbs:

Present	Present Participle	Past	Past Participle
bring	bringing	brought	brought
buy	buying	bought	bought
come	coming	came	come
eat	eating	ate	eaten
go	going	went	gone
see	seeing	saw	seen
sit	sitting	sat	sat
take	taking	took	taken
write	writing	wrote	written

Look at the present participle *bringing*. Read the sentence:

I bringing my dog to the beach.

What is missing in the sentence?

A helping verb is missing, such as *am, is, are, was,* or *were*. The sentence should say:

I *am* bringing my dog to the beach.

Name:

Try It

On the lines provided, write the correct form of the irregular verbs to complete each sentence. Include the right kind of helping verb for participles. An example has been done for you.

Example: present, *sit*
Jim ___sits___ on the floor.

1. past, *bring*

   Anne ______________________ her dog to my house.

2. past, *buy*

   I ______________________ a sandwich for lunch.

3. present participle, come

   My grandparents ______________________ to my soccer game today.

4. past participle, *eat*

   I ______________________ twice this afternoon but I am still hungry.

5. present, *go*

   Let's ______________________ to the park.

6. past participle, *see*

   I know I ______________________ that girl before, I just cannot remember where.

7. past participle, *take*

   It ______________________ a long time to get here.

8. past participle, *write*

   The note ______________________ in a secret code.

Name:

Unit 9 Assessment

Part 1.

Listen to each sound that is read to you. Underline the letters that make each sound.

Hint: You will underline more than one pair of letters for some sounds.

1.	ear	er	ir	ph
2.	ea	or	ph	ur
3.	ar	or	er	ir
4.	ea	ear	ur	ir
5.	ea	ear	ur	ar
6.	ea	ph	ur	ear
7.	er	ir	or	ph
8.	ur	er	ea	ir
9.	ar	ur	or	er
10.	ar	ea	or	er

Part 2.

Listen to each word that is read to you. Write each word on the lines provided.

11. ____________________

12. ____________________

13. ____________________

14. ____________________

15. ____________________

16. ____________________

17. ____________________

18. ____________________

19. ____________________

20. ____________________

Name:

Difficult Spellings & r-Controlled Vowels and Sight Words

Part 3.

Write each word from the box that contains a soft *c* in the Soft *c* column.
Write each word from the box that contains a soft *g* in the Soft *g* column.

camper	center	concert	chapter	large
ginger	glance	game	gym	charm
place	ice	twig	germs	magic

21. Soft *c*

22. Soft *g*

Part 4.

Underline the letters that make the sound /er/ in each of the words below.

23. under

24. surf

25. smirk

26. learn

27. hurt

28. western

29. shirt

30. heard

Name:

Difficult Spellings & r-Controlled Vowels and Sight Words

Part 5.

In each row, underline the word that is read to you.

31.	after	again	anything
32.	begin	both	breath
33.	dirt	does	down
34.	farm	father	friend
35.	gather	get	goes
36.	kept	kiss	know
37.	lace	lamp	laugh
38.	made	mother	my
39.	napkin	next	nut
40.	on	one	only
41.	again	anything	are
42.	frame	friend	from

Name:

Difficult Spellings & r-Controlled Vowels and Sight Words

Part 6.

Read each word aloud.

43. anything

44. only

45. next

46. mother

47. laugh

48. know

49. goes

50. friend

51. father

52. down

53. begin

54. after

Spell the Sound

Underline the letters that spell the vowel sound that completes each word. Then write each word on the lines provided. An example has been done for you.

Example:	b____l	oi	oy	boil
1.	t____	oi	oy	________
2.	f____l	oi	oy	________
3.	b____	oi	oy	________
4.	R____	oi	oy	________
5.	c____n	oi	oy	________
6.	p____nt	oi	oy	________
7.	j____	oi	oy	________
8.	____l	oi	oy	________

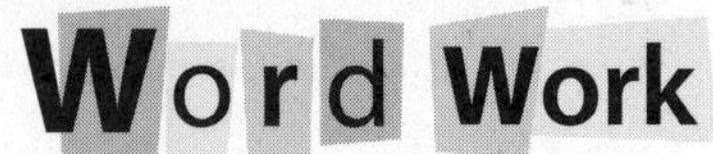

Name:

oi/oy and Sight Words 1

Complete the Sentence

Choose the sight words from the box that best complete each sentence. Write the words on the lines provided. Then read each sentence aloud.

even	mother	gone	look	father	only

1. There is ________________ one hot dog left on the grill.
2. The number six is an ________________ number.
3. My ________________ went to shop for a new skirt.
4. All the cake was ________________ by the time I got to the party.
5. Help me ________________ for my lost cat!
6. Ted's ________________ is a fireman.

Choose two words from the box above. On the lines provided, write each word in a sentence.

7. ____

____

8. ____

____

Name:

oi/oy and Sight Words

Part 3.

Listen to the word that is read to you. Find the word in the sentence. Underline the word.

21. "Will you help Lon look for his bike lock?" Lola asked.

22. "This soil is full of silt," Sol said.

23. Eve said to Earl, "If we both have one slice of cake, then we will be even."

24. "All the gold rings were gone by the time I got to the shop," Glen said.

25. Phil said to Roy, "Cover that can full of fat with foil."

26. Tom said to Tim, "Put that top in the toy box."

Part 4.

Listen to each sentence that is read to you. Write the sentences on the lines provided.

27. ____________________

____

28. ____________________

____

29. ____________________

____

30. ____________________

____

Name:

Part 5.

Read each word aloud.

31. soil

32. joy

33. even

34. spoil

35. gone

36. join

37. look

38. coin

39. joint

40. enjoy

Sort the Words

The vowel sound /aw/ can be spelled *au* or *aw*. Write the words from the box in the correct columns below according to how the sound /aw/ is spelled.

taut	lawn	August	awful	launch
author	sauce	yawn	straw	claw
fawn	crawl	haul	hawk	haunted

au	***aw***

Choose one *au* word and one *aw* word from the box above. On the lines provided, write each word in a sentence.

1. ______________________________

2. ______________________________

Name:

au/aw **and Sight Words 1**

Spell It!

In each row, underline the letter that completes the word. Write the full word on the line provided. Then read each word aloud.

1.	d__es	e	o	a	____________
2.	ver__	t	e	y	____________
3.	do__n	w	r	l	____________
4.	f__ther	o	a	e	____________
5.	so__e	m	s	n	____________
6.	b__gin	i	a	e	____________
7.	__ove	h	b	l	____________
8.	a__ter	n	f	r	____________
9.	lo__k	o	i	n	____________
10.	__nly	a	o	e	____________

Name:

Get Ready

- The *regular* ending for past and past participle verbs is *-d* or *-ed*. For example:

  I *fill* the glass. (present)

  I *filled* the glass. (past)

  I *have filled* the glass. (past participle)

- Past and past participle forms of *irregular verbs* do *not* end in *-d* or *-ed*. For example:

  I *eat* an apple. (present)

  I *ate* an apple. (past)

  I *have eaten* an apple. (past participle)

- Below is a list of common irregular verbs and their present, past, and past participle forms.

Present	Past	Past Participle
bring	brought	(have) brought
come	came	(have) come
do	did	(have) done
eat	ate	(have) eaten
give	gave	(have) given
go	went	(have) gone
is (am, are)	was (were)	(have) been
make	made	(have) made
see	saw	(have) seen
sit	sat	(have) sat
take	took	(have) taken
sing	sang	(have) sung

Name:

au/aw and Sight Words 1

Try It

Write the missing forms of each regular or irregular verb on the lines provided.

	Present	Past	Past Participle
1.	walk	______	(have) walked
2.	drip	dripped	(have) ______
3.	see	______	(have) seen
4.	______	baked	(have) baked
5.	come	came	(have) ______
6.	______	sat	(have) sat
7.	give	______	(have) given
8.	work	worked	(have) ______
9.	______	took	(have) taken
10.	walk	______	(have) walked

Unit 11 Assessment

Part 1.

Listen to each word that is read to you. Write the words on the lines provided.

1. ________________
2. ________________
3. ________________
4. ________________
5. ________________
6. ________________
7. ________________
8. ________________
9. ________________
10. ________________

☼ Assessment

Name:

***au/aw* and Sight Words**

Part 2.

Listen to each word that is read to you. In each word, underline the letters that make the vowel sound in that word.

11. au aw

12. au aw

13. au aw

14. au aw

15. au aw

Part 3.

Choose the word from the box that best completes each sentence. Write the words on the lines provided. Then read each sentence aloud.

haunted	love	very	draw	fawn

16. Jess likes to ______________ with a black ink pen.

17. "I ______________ you so much!" the mother said to her child.

18. They say that the old cabin by the lake is ______________ .

19. "That is a ______________ old coin," the bank clerk said.

20. The ______________ got lost in the forest.

Name:

au/aw **and Sight Words**

Part 4.

In each row, underline the word that is read to you.

21.	stall	straw	strong
22.	lawn	lunch	launch
23.	love	have	live
24.	away	awning	awful
25.	top	taut	trot
26.	haunted	handed	hunted
27.	ever	very	were
28.	crawl	call	caw
29.	hack	honk	hawk
30.	Sam	some	sin

Name:

au/aw **and Sight Words**

Part 5.

In each row, underline the letters that complete the word. Write the full word on the line provided. Then say the word aloud.

31. y___n au aw ____________

32. cl___ au aw ____________

33. f___lt au aw ____________

34. ___ful au aw ____________

35. h___l au aw ____________

36. str___ au aw ____________

37. ___thor au aw ____________

38. s___ce au aw ____________

39. h___k au aw ____________

40. ___gust Au Aw ____________

Name:

ow/ou and Sight Words 1

Spell It!

Write each word from the box in the correct column below according to how the sound /ou/ is spelled — *ow* or *ou*.

brown	round	mound	gown	frown
sound	plow	proud	aloud	how
cow	crouch	now	crowd	cloud
town	couch	found	towel	down
slouch	drown	clown	loud	grouch

ow	***ou***

Name:

ow/ou **and Sight Words 1**

Complete the Sentence

Choose the sight words from the box that best complete each sentence below. Write the words on the lines provided. Then read each sentence aloud.

none	love	more	very
someone	held	even	look

1. Do you want ____________ or less shrimp for lunch?
2. Buzz is ____________ late. He will miss the show.
3. Mom and I went to a shop downtown to ____________ for new dresses.
4. Dad ____________ my hand as we crossed the street.
5. What sports do you and your friends ____________ most?
6. You can not have a pop. There are ____________ left in the box.
7. Fred, ____________ is here to see you. He did not tell me his name.
8. She frowned ____________ more when I told her the bad news.

Complete the sentence below with three words from the box above. Write the words on the lines provided.

9. I ____________ my dog ____________ much, ____________ when she barks a lot.

Find the /ou/ Word

Read the sentences aloud. In each sentence, find the word that contains the sound /ou/. Write the word on the line provided. Then read the sentences aloud again.

1. There is a brand new park in my town.

 ____

2. "Do not be a grouch or we will not be friends!"

 ____

3. Let us be proud of our grand land!

 ____

4. Mr. Neff plants on his farm with a plow.

 ____

5. The crowd loved the rock band and its fun songs.

 ____

6. The cat crouched near the bird that fell from its nest.

 ____

7. Did the wedding gown have lots of lace?

 ____

8. At sunset, the clouds looked pink and red.

 ____

Study, Cover, and Spell: Sight Words

Read each word and then cover it up so that you cannot see it. Spell the word out loud, and then write the word on the line provided. Uncover the word and check your spelling. If it does not match, erase the word and write it again.

1. none ____________
2. very ____________
3. some ____________
4. held ____________
5. even ____________
6. love ____________
7. more ____________
8. only ____________
9. know ____________

Unit 12 Assessment

Part 1.

Say each word below aloud. Underline the sound *ow* or *ou* makes in each word.

1.	grow	/ou/	/ō/
2.	plow	/ou/	/ō/
3.	cloud	/ou/	/ō/
4.	slow	/ou/	/ō/
5.	brown	/ou/	/ō/
6.	mound	/ou/	/ō/
7.	town	/ou/	/ō/
8.	row	/ou/	/ō/
9.	house	/ou/	/ō/
10.	flow	/ou/	/ō/

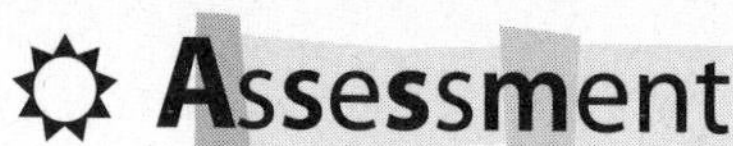

Name:

ow/ou and Sight Words

Part 2.

Listen to each word that is read to you. Write each word on the lines provided.

11. ____________________

12. ____________________

13. ____________________

14. ____________________

15. ____________________

16. ____________________

17. ____________________

18. ____________________

19. ____________________

20. ____________________

Name:

ow/ou **and Sight Words**

Part 3.

In each row, underline the word that contains the long *o* sound.

21.	sled	slow	slot
22.	glow	gown	grade
23.	crow	clown	cross
24.	flag	flow	flower
25.	ship	sound	show
26.	brick	brown	blown
27.	shadow	shade	should
28.	take	throw	three
29.	wound	window	where
30.	snow	stand	shot

Name:

ow/ou **and Sight Words**

Part 4.

In each row, underline the word that is read to you.

31.	would	should	could
32.	held	hand	hop
33.	mouse	mow	more
34.	would	should	could
35.	vet	very	vow
36.	would	should	could
37.	shout	should	shed
38.	now	none	no
39.	hill	hole	held
40.	could	cloud	cloth
41.	where	what	would
42.	mouth	more	saw

Part 5.

Read each word aloud.

43. none
44. would
45. held
46. should
47. more
48. could
49. even
50. love
51. some
52. would
53. should
54. could

Name:

Principal Parts of Verbs

Get Ready

- There are four principal forms of verbs:

  1. present **2.** present participle **3.** past **4.** past participle

- These four sentences show the principal forms of the verb, *play*.

  Present: I *play* softball.

  Present Participle: I *am playing* softball now.

  Past: I *played* softball yesterday.

  Past Participle: I *have played* softball all my life.

- For the *present* tense, just use a main verb.

  I *jump*.

- For the *present participle*, add *–ing* to the main verb. Add a helping verb such as *am*, *are*, *was*, or *were*.

  I *am jumping* now.

- For the *past*, just add the ending *–ed* to the main verb.

  I *jumped* yesterday.

- For the *past participle* of regular verbs, add the ending *–ed* to the main verb. Add a helping verb such as *has*, *have*, or *had*.
  Remember: Helping verbs go before a main verb.

  I *have jumped* for a long time.

Name:

Try It

On the line provided in each sentence, write the correct form of the *main verb* in parentheses.

1. Tess fell and (land) ________________ on the ground.
2. Jeff has (live) ________________ in his house for ten months.
3. The frog was (hop) ________________ into and out of the pond.
4. I had (hope) ________________ for a new bike for my birthday.

Read each sentence below. Write the correct verb on the line provided.
Hint: When you see the word *participle*, add a helping verb to the main verb of the sentence.

5. Mom (past of *frown*) ________________ when she saw the mess.
6. The band (present participle of *play*) ________________ right now, so let's dance.
7. The cat (past participle of *drag*) ________________ ________________ a mouse into the house.
8. We (present of *plow*) ________________ the land to grow corn.
9. It (past participle of *snow*) ________________ ________________ for many months.
10. The wind (present participle of *blow*) ________________ and it is very cold.

Name:

Long *a* and Sight Words 1

Choose the Spelling

Underline the long *a* spelling that completes each word. Write the full word on the line provided. Then say the words aloud.

1. cl__ ai ay ________________
2. p__nt ai ay ________________
3. tr__ ai ay ________________
4. ch__n ai ay ________________
5. r__n ai ay ________________
6. s__ ai ay ________________
7. gr__ ai ay ________________
8. st__n ai ay ________________

Choose the words from above that best complete each sentence below. Write the words on the lines provided.

9. The red ________________ dripped off the brush onto the rug.
10. Grace wears a gold ________________.
11. The ________________ came down all ________________.

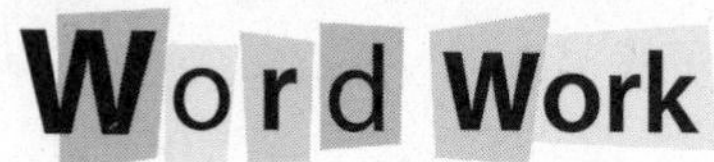

Name:

Long *a* and Sight Words 1

By Sight

See how many words you can read correctly in one minute. Read aloud across the rows. When you get to the bottom of the page, start over. Try to read more words the second time.

look	none	father	some	could
laugh	would	love	more	out
friend	next	should	gone	very
mother	held	even	again	only
look	very	some	would	friend
could	father	more	next	none
love	gone	laugh	held	mother
again	out	only	should	even

Number of words read correctly: ______

Underline the words *would*, *could*, and *should* above.
Hint: Each word appears twice.

A bird that was in the tree outside the window flew into my room. It landed on my head. It was scared and kept flapping its wings. Mom came running upstairs to see what the ruckus was about. Dad got up off the tarp. He had yellow paint all over his head. He looked like a big smiley face! I was flailing my hands about like a madman. I was trying to get the bird out of my hair. Mom started to giggle. She couldn't stop! She giggled so much that she didn't even get mad about the cracked window! All I can say is that I'm glad we used a tarp. That yellow paint would have left a big stain on the rug. And the next time we paint, I'll be sure Angel is not inside our house!

Wet Paint

Yay! I get to paint my room today! First we moved my bed, desk, and chair into the hallway. Then we put tape around anything that didn't need to get painted. I put tape around the window. Dad put tape around the door. The last thing we did was put a plastic tarp over the carpet. That way we could drip paint and it wouldn't matter.

Now we were ready to start painting. Dad let me open the paint can. I used

a screwdriver to take off the lid. POP! I used a stick to stir the paint. It was so yellow! I was afraid it might be too yellow. But Dad said it would look okay later when it dried on the walls. I sure hoped so!

Dad poured some of the paint into a pair of trays. Then he gave me a brush.

He fixed his tray to the ladder. Dad started to paint near the top of a wall. I painted down low, near the floor. We worked our way around the room. We made a good team!

At last Dad and I were done. I was glad, too. I was getting a pain in my arm. Dad came down from the ladder. He stepped back to see if we missed any spots. YEOW! Dad had stepped on Angel's tail! Angel is a stray cat. "How did she get in here?" shouted Dad. Angel let out a howl and ran out the door. She hit the paint can on the way out. It fell over with a crash. Paint went all over the place! Dad took a step and slipped on the paint. He fell down hard. He hit the ladder with his leg. The ladder tipped over. It fell into the window. CRASH!

Name:

Long *a* and Sight Words 2

Give Me an A!

In each sentence, find the word that has the long *a* sound. Then write the word on the line provided.

1. The man had to rake the sand.

    ____

2. That apron has a tan band at the top.

    ____

3. Fran saw the flame of a candle in the dark.

    ____

4. Brad asked if he could have some cake.

    ____

5. Tad planted an acorn in the backyard.

    ____

6. My pal, April, has a bad cold.

    ____

7. Jack slammed the backyard gate shut.

    ____

8. Matt can help Jan, but he is not able to help Mark.

    ____

Name:

Long *a* and Sight Words 2

Can You See Them?

Underline the sight word listed as many times as it appears in each row. An example has been done for you.

Example:	brother	other	brother	mother	bother	brother
1.	could	could	cold	would	could	cold
2.	sister	sitter	silver	sister	sitter	sister
3.	none	gone	none	some	none	some
4.	baby	baby	maybe	only	barb	baby
5.	would	should	would	should	could	would
6.	brother	other	brother	brother	bother	other
7.	more	more	none	mare	more	mine
8.	should	shout	shock	should	shout	should
9.	held	help	held	held	helm	help

Get Ready

- The time of a verb's action or being is called its *tense*. The basic verb tenses are *present*, *past*, and *future*.

Present singular:	The cow *jumps* over the moon.
Present plural:	The cows *jump* over the moon.
Past singular:	The cow *jumped* over the moon.
Past plural:	The cows *jumped* over the moon.
Future singular:	The cow *will jump* over the moon.
Future plural:	The cows *will jump* over the moon

Note that the past form of an *irregular* verb does **not** end in *-d* or *-ed*.

Past singular:	I *saw* the cow jump over the moon.
Past plural:	We *saw* the cow jump over the moon.

- The *present* or *past progressive* tense shows *continuous action* or *being*.

We make the present progressive tense by adding a present tense helping verb (*am*, *is*, or *are*) to the present participle of a verb.

Present progressive singular:	The cow *is jumping* over the moon.
Present progressive plural:	The cows *are jumping* over the moon.

We make the past progressive tense by adding a past tense helping verb (*was* or *were*) to the present participle of a verb.

Past progressive singular:	The cow *was jumping* over the moon.
Past progressive plural:	The cows *were jumping* over the moon.

Name:

Long *a* and Sight Words 2

Try It

Underline the correct verb tense that completes each sentence.

1. Yesterday I (go, went) to the hat shop.
2. Bob (has , have) a pet pig.
3. Brent was (running , runs) in the big race when it started to rain.
4. Jack (taken, took) my sister to the dance.
5. The cat is (plays, playing) with the ball of string.
6. Don and I (was, were) the first two kids in line for the show.

Choose the verb from the box that best completes each sentence. Write each verb on the lines provided.
Hint: Not all the words in the box are used.

trips	says	flip	sitting	ate
sits	eat	sat	were	tripped
eaten	are	was	trip	am

7. Jake ________________ over that rock yesterday. Be careful that you don't ________________ over it today!
8. Chuck ________________ cake today, but I will ________________ cake tomorrow.
9. Marla ________________ in the van. I am ________________ next to her.
10. We ________________ singing while Pat ________________ dancing.

Name:

Long *a* and Sight Words 3

Which Word?

Choose the word from the box that best completes each sentence below. Write the words on the lines provided.

weight	sleigh	great	eight
break	freight	steak	weigh

1. How much does that box of crackers ________________?
2. Pete wants to grill a ________________ for dinner.
3. "When will the ________________ train be here?" Greg asked the clerk.
4. Let's take a ________________ from this hard work!
5. Those dogs will pull the ________________.
6. "I have a ________________ idea!" Carlos shouted to his sister.
7. Frank has six toy cars and Elvis has ________________.
8. Alan used the scale to check the ________________ of the box.

Sight Word Scramble

Unscramble each sight word. Write the unscrambled words on the lines provided.

1. yabb ______________
2. treiss ______________
3. herbtro ______________

Use the sight words you unscrambled above to complete the sentences below. Write each word on the lines provided.

4. My ______________ is a Boy Scout.
5. Mother put the ______________ in the crib for a nap.
6. My ______________ won a girls' surfing contest.

On the lines provided, write a sentence using each sight word you unscrambled above.

7. ____

____

8. ____

____

9. ____

____

Would she do it? Would she race Wade? Could she win? That would be great!

"No, that's too far," April said. "How about a race from here to the big acorn tree, and then back again? That's about how far I ran when I won this ribbon." Everyone nodded. That sounded fair. Now they all looked at Wade. What would he say? Wade drew a line in the dirt with the heel of his sneaker. April and Wade lined up. Ready, set, go! Wade ran like a bullet. He got to the acorn tree long before April. But then Wade started to get tired. He had to slow down. But April had paced herself. She knew not to use all of her energy at the start of the race. April flew by Wade on the way back. Wade bent over in pain. He had a cramp. April won the race! Hooray for April! Too bad for Wade!

The Race

A bully lives on my block. His name is Wade. Wade picks on anyone he can. He mocks. He pokes. He pulls hair. No one likes to be around Wade much. One day, Wade heard April talking to her friends. She had just won a blue ribbon the day before. She got it for being the fastest runner in a race. It made Wade mad. Wade wanted the ribbon. "I bet I can beat you," Wade said to April. "I bet you can't run as fast as me." Wade poked his

finger in April's arm. "You know I can run faster than you can."

"Whatever you say," April replied. She was smart. April knew that she should just ignore Wade. April turned her back and went on talking with her friends. But that didn't stop Wade. He kept mocking April. Then he started to pull at one of her braids.

"Come on! Let's race! Let's do it now!" Wade shouted. "What are you? Chicken?

Afraid I'll win? I bet you're afraid that you'll have to give me that ribbon! Poor baby! She's so scared!" Wade tried to grab the ribbon out of April's hand. April's brother stopped him.

"Chill out, Wade," Gabe said as he put out his arm. "Leave my sister alone," he said in a stern way. Gabe gave Wade a grave look. "Why don't you go play with your own friends?" But that didn't stop Wade, because Wade was a bully. He couldn't stop!

"I bet you would look like a snail compared to me!" Wade shouted. "I'm the fastest runner in this town," he bragged. "I deserve that ribbon!"

"Why not race around the lake?" Gail shouted. "That would settle it!" All the kids looked at her. Then they looked at April.

© 2010 K12 Inc. All rights reserved.

Name:

Long *a* and Sight Words 4

Find the Sound

Read aloud the words in the box. Underline the letter or letters that make the long *a* sound in each word.

trail	tray	mail	able
April	Kay	payday	haystack
stain	acorn	apron	strain

Read and Sort

Write the words from the box above in the correct columns below according to how the long *a* sound is spelled in each word.

a	*ai*	*ay*

Name:

Spell It!

In each row, circle the letter that completes the word. Write the full word on the line provided. Then say each word aloud.

1.	br__ther	o	u	e	____________
2.	anim__ls	i	a	e	____________
3.	ma__y	t	n	v	____________
4.	hel__	b	t	d	____________
5.	si__ter	s	n	a	____________
6.	n__ne	e	a	o	____________
7.	w__ile	a	h	o	____________
8.	__ome	s	t	k	____________
9.	__aby	m	l	b	____________
10.	co__ld	u	o	i	____________

Unit 13 Assessment

Part 1.

Listen to each word that is read to you. Write the words on the lines provided.

1. ____________________
2. ____________________
3. ____________________
4. ____________________
5. ____________________
6. ____________________

Part 2.

Read the words below. In each word, underline the letter or letters that make the long *a* sound.

7. plain
8. sway
9. acorn
10. weigh
11. ate
12. able
13. pancake
14. hail

Name:

Long *a* and Sight Words

Part 3.

Read each word in the box. Write the words in the correct columns below according to their spelling of the long *a* sound.

break	age	brain	face
stay	aim	bay	paint
sleigh	play	weight	outbreak
shame	great	nail	make

15. ***a*-consonant-*e***

______
______
______
______

16. ***ai***

______
______
______
______

17. ***ay***

______
______
______
______

18. ***ea***

______
______
______
______

19. ***eigh***

______
______
______
______

☼ Assessment

Name:

Long *a* and Sight Words

Part 4.

Choose the word from the box that best completes each sentence. Write the words on the lines provided.

while	should	many	would
sleigh	baby	brother	animals

20. Brent held his cat ________________ the vet gave it a shot.

21. What ________________ you like for lunch?

22. The ________________ played in her crib.

23. There are ________________ kinds of rocks in this display.

24. It is fun to ride in a ________________ through the snow.

25. My ________________ likes to hike down this trail.

26. There are lots of ________________ in the forest.

27. You ________________ never walk across this path without checking for cars.

Name:

Long *a* and Sight Words

Part 5.

In each row, underline the word that is read to you.

28.	brother	both	bother
29.	wand	world	would
30.	weigh	wade	wane
31.	sits	sister	sitter
32.	shod	shoulder	should
33.	wide	while	whine
34.	many	mane	manner
35.	above	able	about
36.	baby	bade	babble
37.	anvils	anyone	animals
38.	ball	bail	bell
39.	cold	cud	could

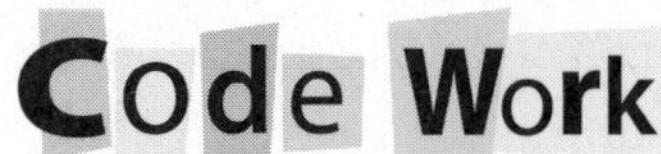

Name:

Long *i* and Sight Words 1

Practice Long *i*

Choose the word from the box that best completes each sentence.
Write each word on the lines provided.

child	find	hind	kind	wild

1. Another word for nice is ______________.
2. A lion is an example of a ______________ animal.
3. An animal's back legs are called its ______________ legs.
4. Can you help me ______________ my book?
5. A person is a ______________ before he or she becomes an adult.

Choose two words from the box above. Write each word in a sentence on the lines provided below.

6. ____

____

7. ____

____

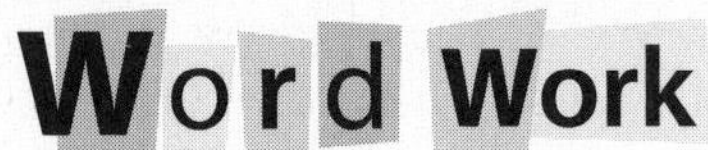

Name:

Long *i* and Sight Words 1

Complete the Sentences

Choose the word from the box that best completes each sentence. Write each word on the lines provided. Then read each sentence aloud.
Hint: One word will be used in two sentences.

animals	many	other
people	while	together

1. We walked to the park ________________ .
2. Frank ate a snack ________________ Mom made a call.
3. How ________________ brothers and sisters do you have?
4. I found one sock but I cannot find the ________________ one.
5. Look at the crowd of ________________ outside of the shop!
6. I sat on a bench ________________ my sister tossed a ball.
7. Some ________________ sleep all day and are awake at night.

Get Ready

- A *verb* tells what someone or something does or is. *Action verbs* show action you can see (*dance, swim, jump*), or action that is mental and invisible (*think, wonder, imagine*). *Being verbs* don't show action but they tell something about what the subject is.

  Max *is* strong and brave.

  Soccer and field hockey *are* my favorite sports.

  Many verbs have two parts: a *main verb* and a *helping verb*. A helping verb does exactly what its name says—it helps the main verb.

  Our family *is driving* to North Carolina.

  Helping verb: *is*

  Main verb: *driving*

  Main verbs can have more than one helping verb.

  We *have been sitting* in the car for a long time.

  Helping verbs: *have been*

  Main verb: *sitting*

  Here are some common helping verbs: *am, was, has, will, is, were, have, can, are, been, had, might, be.*

  There are four principal forms of verbs:

  1. *Present*: shows action or being happening now and does not use a helping verb.
  2. *Present Participle*: ends in *–ing* and uses a helping verb: *am*, *is*, *are*, *was*, or *were*.
  3. *Past*: regular verbs end in *–d* or *–ed*, shows action or being in the past, and does *not* use a helping verb.
  4. *Past Participle*: regular verbs end in *–d* or *–ed*, shows action or being in the past, and uses a helping verb: *has*, *have*, or *had*.

Name:

Try It

Underline the verbs in each sentence.

1. I was late this morning.
2. The dog ran after the cat.
3. How long were you out of town?
4. My best friend lives across the street from me.

On the lines provided, write your own action verbs or being verbs to complete the sentences.

5. Blake ________________ my brother.
6. We ________________ on the same soccer team.
7. I ________________ Ming is older than Bill, but I am not sure.
8. How fast can you ________________ around the track?

In the sentences below, underline the *main verbs* and circle the *helping verbs*. Remember that a main verb can have more than one helping verb.

9. I will walk to the park tomorrow.
10. Kim is helping me with my project.
11. I am going to the fair this weekend.
12. Jeff has been saving his money all summer.

Practice Long *i*

Choose the word from the box that best completes each sentence. Write each word on the lines provided.

pie	cried	lie	spied	tie

1. Who ate all of the ____________?
2. The child ____________ when his toy broke.
3. Mom's head hurt so she went to ____________ down.
4. The baseball game ended in a ____________.
5. Jon ____________ on his sister and her friends.

Choose two words from the box above. On the lines provided below, write a sentence using each word. Then read each sentence aloud.

6. ____

____

7. ____

____

Name:

Sight Words Scramble

Unscramble each sight word. Write each unscrambled word on the lines provided.

1. aailmns ____________
2. eeolpp ____________
3. aymn ____________
4. reeoghtt ____________
5. eohrt ____________
6. eihlw ____________

Writing Sentences

On the lines provided below, write a sentence for each sight word given above.

7. ______________________________
8. ______________________________
9. ______________________________
10. ______________________________
11. ______________________________
12. ______________________________

"I'm sure it will be OK," his sister was quick to say. "It's not like that would stop you from acting on stage. Anyway, would that be so bad?" Jake gave her a shocked look. "Think about it," Kay said. "If they put a cast on your arm, then you won't be able to wash dishes. I know how you hate that job of yours," she said. "And you won't have to write that term paper! How can you type with a bad wrist?" Jake had to laugh.

"You sure have a way of turning rain into a rainbow," he said as he hiked up the slate walkway to their house.

"And where did you get that quaint saying?" Kay joked. "Grandma?"

"You bet!" Jake said. "And I think she really knew what she was talking about!"

Give Me a Break

"Ouch!" Jake yelled. He was sitting on the sidewalk. His skateboard lay next to him. "I think I just sprained my wrist," he said to Kay.

"No way!" Kay shouted. "I told you to wear your pads!" Kay said as she rode her skateboard over to her brother. "Let me see it." Jake held out his left arm. His wrist was turning red. Kay lightly touched his wrist. "Does that hurt?" she asked. Jake pursed his lips and nodded his head.

"What a shame," she said. "But you are lucky you did not break your neck!" she said. "That was some fall." She gave him a sad look. "Are you in a lot of pain?" Jake nodded again. Kay frowned. "I'm sorry." She helped Jake stand up. "We better get you home right away. You will have to get an X-ray." Jake went for his skateboard

with his good hand. "No, let me take your board," Kay said. She picked it up and they started to walk home. Jake held his left wrist with his right hand. He was doing his best not to cry.

Kay kept talking to keep Jake's mind off the pain. "So, did I tell you about the email I got?" she asked. "I found out I'm one of the eight kids who gets to paint the scenery for the play." She had a big grin on her face. Kay was a great artist. "I heard over fifty kids wanted that job."

"Oh, no!" shouted Jake. "I'm in the play! But how can I act with a sprained wrist?" Jake forgot all about the pain he was in. Now he was worried about losing his part as the evil Mr. Gray. "What if I broke a bone? What if I have to get a cast?" Jake asked. "This day is going from bad to worse."

Name:

Long *i* and Sight Words 3

The Long *i* Sound

Write each word from the box in the correct column below according to how the long *i* sound is spelled in each word. Then write one word of your own in each column.

bright	child	cries
dried	find	grind
high	tie	tight

i	***igh***	***ie***

Choose one word from each column above. On the lines provided below, write a sentence using each word. Then read each sentence aloud.

1. ______________________________

____

2. ______________________________

____

3. ______________________________

____

Complete the Sentences

Choose the word from the box that best completes each sentence. Write each word on the lines provided. Then read each sentence aloud.
Hint: One word will be used in two sentences.

above	here	move
other	people	together

1. I hung the poster ________________ my desk.
2. Many ________________ ride the bus every day.
3. When did they ________________ to Ohio?
4. Pete and Will played games ________________ all afternoon.
5. Would you like me to put the box ________________ or there?
6. I cannot ________________ the table because it is too heavy.
7. Bella closed one window but her cat jumped out of the ________________ one.

Practice Long *i*

Choose the word from the box that best completes each sentence. Write each word on the lines provided. Then underline the letters that make the long *i* sound in each word. An example has been done for you.

dime	child	right	pie	high
die	ice	wild	night	nine

Example: Without water and sunlight, plants will __die__.

1. Frozen water is ____________.
2. A ____________ is a kind of dessert.
3. A ____________ grows into an adult.
4. The opposite of left is ____________.
5. The opposite of low is ____________.
6. The opposite of day is ____________.
7. If an animal is not tame, it is ____________.
8. The number before ten is ____________.
9. A ____________ is worth ten cents.

By Sight

See how many words you can read correctly in one minute. Read aloud across the rows. When you get to the bottom of the page, start over. Try to read more words correctly the second time.

above	many	would	love	mother
here	animals	know	very	gone
move	while	together	some	only
other	brother	none	even	down
should	sister	more	look	after
people	baby	held	father	could

Number of words read correctly: _____

One hot day, Mike went wading in the pond. He looked for Birdie, but didn't see him anywhere. Then Mike saw something move on the sand near some small rocks. Sunshine ran over to the rocks. She sniffed at some small, cracked eggs. Mike went over to take a look. Mike saw six baby turtles on the sand! Then he saw two more swimming in the water. That's when Mike figured out that Birdie was a girl. "I think I might change Birdie's name again," Mike said when he got home. "Birdie is a girl." Mom and Dad didn't say anything for a moment. Then Mom spoke up.

"How about Myrtle?" she said.

"Myrtle the Turtle," said Mike. "I like it!" And that's been her name ever since.

What Is in a Name?

Mike has a new friend. It's a turtle! The turtle lives in the pond by Mike's house. One day, Mike was sailing his toy boat on the pond. That's when he first saw the turtle. It was sitting high above his head on a big rock. It was staring at Mike and his dog. Mike's dog is named Sunshine. Sunshine had never seen a turtle before. The sight of the turtle filled Sunshine with fright. She started to bark. The turtle got scared and

© 2010 K12 Inc. All rights reserved.

tucked its head, legs, and tail inside its shell. That's why Mike named the turtle Tucker. "Tucker likes to tuck inside his shell. He's funny," Mike told his mom.

Mike wanted to bring Tucker home as a pet. But his dad said that Tucker was a wild turtle. "He shouldn't live here.

Tucker should stay by the pond," said Dad. So Mike and Sunshine would visit Tucker whenever they had the time. Mike would sit and talk to Tucker. Tucker didn't seem to mind. He just sat in the bright sunlight and listened. Tucker was a very kind turtle!

One day Tucker came very close to Mike. Mike got to look at the stripes and spots on the turtle's shell. Then Tucker opened his mouth wide. Mike was surprised. Tucker didn't have any teeth! Later that day, Dad told Mike that turtles have a beak instead of teeth. They use their beaks to catch and eat food. Dad said to be careful because Tucker might bite. Mike said that the turtle's beak made him think of a bird. So he changed Tucker's name to Birdie.

Unit 14 Assessment

Part 1.

Read each word below. On the lines provided, write *Y* for *yes* if the word contains the long *i* sound. Write *N* for *no* if the word does not contain the long *i* sound.

1. strings ______
2. blinded ______
3. strides ______
4. blinked ______
5. slight ______
6. flips ______
7. flies ______
8. sunlight ______
9. chilled ______
10. finds ______

Part 2.

Listen to each word that is read to you. Write each word on the lines provided.

11. ______________
12. ______________
13. ______________
14. ______________
15. ______________
16. ______________
17. ______________
18. ______________
19. ______________
20. ______________

Name:

Long *i* and Sight Words

Part 3.

In each row, underline the word that contains the long *i* sound.

21. kind kids kissed
22. skin skies skips
23. sight sir stink
24. tries trips tricks
25. think things thigh
26. shift shine ships
27. ticked tips tied
28. find finish fins
29. fist fight figs
30. girls ginger grinds

Assessment

Name:

Long *i* and Sight Words

Part 4.

In each row, underline the word that is read to you.

31.	after	animals	above
32.	against	anything	again
33.	here	held	her
34.	many	move	mother
35.	now	none	next
36.	out	only	other
37.	put	pull	people
38.	they	there	that
39.	together	too	their
40.	are	against	and
41.	north	napkin	now
42.	the	there	them

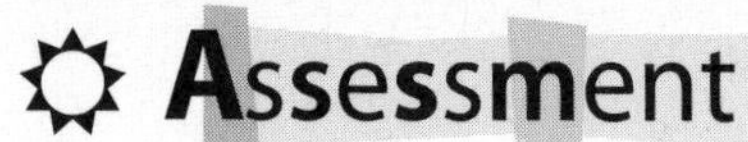

Name:

Long *i* and Sight Words

Part 5.

Read each word aloud.

43. together

44. there

45. people

46. other

47. she

48. now

49. move

50. here

51. against

52. above

53. there

54. now

55. against

Name:

Get Ready

- **Adjectives** are words that describe nouns.

One of the most common ways adjectives describe nouns is that they describe *what kind***.**

a *fast* car	What kind of car (noun)?	*fast* (adjective)
a *great* day	What kind of day (noun)?	*great* (adjective)
a *funny* joke	What kind of joke (noun)?	*funny* (adjective)

Many times, an adjective appears in a sentence before the noun it describes.

The *old* **mug** was filled with *hot* **tea**.

However, when the main verb of a sentence is a *being verb*, any adjective that describes the subject will probably follow the verb.

The **day** was *gray* and *rainy*.

Adjectives can make writing much more interesting by adding descriptive and lively details that help a reader see things more clearly.

That dog is *mine*.

That *spotted, friendly* dog is *mine.*

Name:

Try It

On the lines provided, label each word as either an adjective (**A**) or a noun (**N**).

1. ______ exciting

2. ______ wild

3. ______ teacup

4. ______ shoe

5. ______ sharp

6. ______ train

7. ______ chicken

8. ______ green

9. ______ pretzel

10. ______ scared

11. ______ bluebird

12. ______ loud

13. ______ skateboard

14. ______ snake

15. ______ confused

16. ______ movie

17. ______ spotted

18. ______ cobweb

On the lines provided, write five adjective + noun pairs using the adjectives and nouns from above. An example has been done for you.

Example: spotted teacup

19. ______________________

20. ______________________

21. ______________________

22. ______________________

23. ______________________

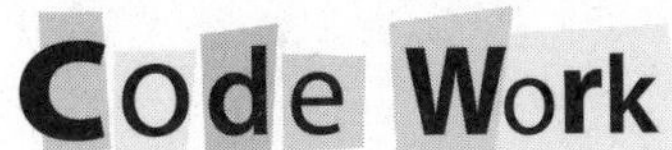

Name:

Practice Long *o*

Underline each word in the box that contains the long *o* sound, as in *go*.

hello	cow	over	row	plow
how	open	flow	plot	stow
sold	porch	storm	tow	told
glow	bold	fork	stop	snow

On the lines provided, write two words that contain the long *o* sound spelled *o* (choose words *not* shown in the box above).

1. ______________________

2. ______________________

On the lines provided, write two words that contain the long *o* sound spelled *ow* (choose words *not* shown in the box above).

3. ______________________

4. ______________________

Name:

Long *o* and Sight Words 1

By Sight

See how many words you can read correctly in one minute. Read aloud across the rows. When you get to the last word, start over. Try to read more words the second time.

now	many	together	above	there
animals	move	people	sister	huge
while	brother	there	above	sister
many	against	together	people	animals
other	huge	baby	brother	against
while	now	other	baby	move

Number of words read correctly: ______

Word Finder

Underline the words *there*, *against*, and *now* in the rows above.

what it was. Then I heard the low sound of an engine. I looked up. A car was coming down the highway. Just then, Old Mo shot out of the tree and stayed low to the ground. He dropped the walnut on the blacktop. Then he dashed back up to the walnut tree and waited. As the car drove by, it ran over the walnut and cracked it open. When the car was gone, Old Mo shot back down to the highway. He walked over to the cracked walnut. Then he picked up his snack with his bill and ate it. I was shocked! "So that's where all those broken nutshells come from!" I shouted. "Old Mo, you are one smart bird!" Old Mo turned his head and looked at me. You know, to this day I swear that bird gave me a wink before he spread his wings to fly away.

Old Mo

An old crow lives on our farm. He's been here since my dad was a boy. We call him Old Mo. His feathers are as black as tar, just like my Uncle Mo's hair. That is how Old Mo got his name.

There are times when I think Old Mo is my shadow. No matter where I go, there's Old Mo. In the spring, I see Old Mo fly over my head while I sow row after row of corn. In the summer, I see Old Mo standing on our dock while I throw

rocks in the pond. In the fall, I see Old Mo sitting in the old walnut tree while I mow the hay. In the winter, I see Old Mo walking on the snow while I put sacks of winter beans on the truck.

I see Old Mo over and over, so I started to talk to him. I don't think he minds. In

fact, I think he knows what I'm saying! When I talk to Old Mo, he starts to caw. It's almost like he's talking back to me. It's nice to have a pal to talk to, even if it is a bird! Now it's like I have a friend by my side when I am working in the fields. And it makes those long days on the farm go by so much faster.

There has always been a mystery on our farm. Once in a while we see cracked nutshells on the highway that leads to town. No one knows where they come from. It's such an odd thing. One October day, I went to stow my rake in the shed. I had just spent all day getting rid of weeds in the pumpkin patch. I could see Old Mo sitting on a branch in the old walnut tree. "Hello, Old Mo!" I said. "How are you today?" I could see that there was something in his mouth. I wondered

Name:

Long *o* and Sight Words 2

One Sound, Two Spellings

Write each word from the box in the correct column below according to the spelling of the long *o* sound.

soap	hoe	potatoes	road	throat
toes	boast	moan	Joe	loaf
foe	soak	toast	toad	croak

oa	***oe***

Name:

Long *o* and Sight Words 2

Sight Words Scramble and Sentences

Unscramble each sight word. Write the unscrambled words on the lines provided.

1. yerev ______________
2. ihednb ______________
3. birengoh ______________

Choose the sight word from above that best completes each sentence. Write the words on the lines provided.
Hint: One word will be used twice.

4. Joan lives next to us so she is our ______________ .
5. ______________ time we need help, she is there.
6. There are nice cooking smells ______________ her door.
7. Our ______________ Joan shares her best dishes with us, too.

Writing Sentences

On the lines provided below, write a sentence for each sight word given above.

8. ______________________________
9. ______________________________
10. ______________________________

Name:

Long *o* and Sight Words 2

Get Ready

- The words *a* and *an* are called *articles*. These short words are a kind of adjective. Like other adjectives, they describe a noun. *A* and *an* describe by telling us that a noun is one of a group or kind of person, place, or thing.

  Mom told us *a* story.

  Jed found *an* egg.

- In English, we use *a* before words that begin with a consonant sound. We use *an* before words that begin with a vowel sound. Notice that it is the first *sound*, not the first *letter*, that tells you which article to use.

  an apple

  a letter

  an hour (The first sound is a vowel sound even though the word *hour* starts with the consonant *h*.)

  a home (The first sound is the consonant *h*.)

Name:

Try It

On the lines provided, write the correct article to use with each word or words: *a* or *an*.

1. _____ cold
2. _____ shadow
3. _____ ant
4. _____ ice cube
5. _____ hour
6. _____ home
7. _____ bowl
8. _____ rowboat
9. _____ phone
10. _____ ape

Name:

Long *o* and Sight Words 3

Find the Right Word

In each sentence, find the word in which the long *o* sound is spelled with the letter *o* and a silent *e*, separated by a consonant. Write the word on the line provided.

1. The old house was made of stone. ______________
2. My dog has a cold, wet nose. ______________
3. I hope the boat will float. ______________
4. Let us go home now. ______________
5. The farmer broke the ground with a hoe. ______________
6. Do not talk on the phone now. ______________

Writing Sentences

Choose two words from above in which the long *o* sound is spelled with the letter *o* and a silent *e*, separated by a consonant. On the lines provided below, write each word in a sentence.

7. ____

____

8. ____

____

Name:

Long *o* and Sight Words 3

Complete the Sentence

Choose the word from the box that best completes each sentence. Write each word on the lines provided.
Note: Each word will be used twice.

every	behind	neighbor

1. We read a book ______________ night.

2. Do not get ______________ in your homework.

3. Our ______________ helped us cut our tree down.

4. Do you play baseball ______________ spring?

5. Please take this loaf of bread to our ______________ .

6. My brother sat ______________ me on the bus.

down in a plush chair near the cozy fire. Burt lay on a nearby rug and chewed on a bone. "How would you like to hear a story about a boy who takes a trip down the Nile River?" Sir Poe asked Burt. Once again, Burt blew smoke out of his nose. Burt was happy! Let's go!

Dragon Tale

Sir Poe looked out at his kingdom from the tower window. Every single thing that he could see was his. The land, the trees, the rocks, the animals—they all belonged to Sir Poe. It was a grand kingdom. And it was a grand day. It had been a long, cold winter. There had been days and days of snow. Today was the first sunny day in months. Sir Poe sniffed the air. "Oh, spring! You are my favorite season," he said aloud.

As he looked out the window, Sir Poe saw Burt, his pet dragon. Burt was lying next to the lake. He was enjoying the warm sun. His green scales shined in the light. Sir Poe and Burt had not been on a ride together all winter long. So, Sir

front of the moat. Home at last! Sir Poe stepped off Burt's back. Then he pulled an apple out of his pocket and tossed it into Burt's mouth. Snap! Burt closed his mouth hard and ate the apple in one gulp. Then Sir Poe led Burt across the moat and into the castle for the night.

The castle was very cold inside, now that the sun was gone. Sir Poe brought Burt over to the enormous fireplace. "OK, Burt!" he said. "You know what to do." Burt took a deep breath. Then he blew a stream of flames out of his mouth. It lit the wood in the fireplace in a second. "Thank you, Burt!" said Sir Poe. "Good job!" Sir Poe gave Burt a pat on his thorny head. The dragon smiled at his human friend. Sir Poe hung a kettle full of stew over the fire. Then he went to the table and picked up a book. He sat

© 2010 K12 Inc. All rights reserved.

Burt flew all the way through to the edge of the forest. Now when Sir Poe looked down, he saw the blue ocean far below them. That meant it was time to turn back. He gave Burt a small poke with his big toe. Burt rose high in the air and made a giant turn. Sir Poe looked behind Burt's tail at the sunset. The sky was red and the clouds were orange. When he looked forward again, everything on the land looked like it was made out of gold. Sir Poe's kingdom never looked so wonderful.

At last Sir Poe could see his castle again. He waved at a neighbor as they flew by. Just before they got home, Burt flew over the garden where the roses grow. So many flowers! Sir Poe sniffed the air again. So sweet! In another minute, Burt set down on the ground in

Poe thought today was the perfect time to go for a spin. He put on a long, warm coat and went down the many stone steps to the ground floor of the castle. As he walked through the huge main room, Sir Poe looked at the paintings of his family on the walls. He saw pictures of his aunts and uncles, brothers and sisters, and mother and father. But they were all gone now. They had all died due to war or illness. Only Sir Poe and his pet dragon were left. That is how Sir Poe came to rule the kingdom all by himself.

The heavy door moaned as Sir Poe pushed it open. He walked across the drawbridge that spanned the moat. Sir Poe looked to his side and saw a pair of pink swans floating on the dark water. One of them let out a big honk. That made a toad croak. Just then, a golden fish flew into the air. It did a flip then fell back into the water with a splash. A doe came up to Sir Poe as he walked down the road. Sir Poe reached into his pocket. Then he fed the doe a small bit of bread. A huge, black crow suddenly flew over Sir Poe's head. It let out a loud screech. Sir Poe laughed and gave the crow some bread, too. At last he made it to the lake and Burt. Sir Poe loved all the animals in his kingdom, but he loved his green dragon most of all. "How would you like to go for a ride over the forest?" Sir Poe asked Burt. The dragon lifted his big head and shot smoke out of his nose. Sir Poe knew this meant Burt was happy. Let's go!

Burt bent down so Sir Poe could get on his back. Even though Sir Poe was a full-grown man, he was a light load

for Burt. The dragon spread his silvery wings and leaped into the sky. They started out low. Then they moved up, up, up into the air. Sir Poe looked down below. Everything seemed so small. His huge castle home looked like a toy. The farms looked like the little patches of a quilt. And the river looked like a skinny, blue thread. Sir Poe smiled. What a treat to be able to see the clouds from above! Sir Poe sniffed the air. It smelled very fresh. He knew this meant that they were near the forest. The air always smelled better when they were flying over trees. Burt moved up, down, and through the rows of pines. It was a sort of game of his. Sir Poe held the dragon's neck tight. He enjoyed this part of the ride most of all.

Name:

Long *o* and Sight Words 4

The Long *o* Sound

Write each word from the box in the correct column below according to how the long *o* sound is spelled in each word.

hope	toad	stone	moat	note
foe	road	doe	toe	

o-e	*oa*	*oe*

Writing Sentences

Choose one word from each column above. On the lines provided below, write a sentence using each word. Then read each sentence aloud.

1. ______________________________

____

2. ______________________________

____

3. ______________________________

____

Name:

Long *o* and Sight Words 4

Sight Words Scramble and Sentences

Unscramble each sight word. Write each unscrambled word on the lines provided.

1. roghbein ____________

2. ecno ____________

3. moec ____________

4. eeyrv ____________

5. inhdeb ____________

6. tbaou ____________

On the lines provided below, write each word from above in a sentence. Then read the sentences aloud.

7. ________________________

8. ________________________

9. ________________________

10. ________________________

11. ________________________

12. ________________________

Name:

Unit 15 Assessment

Part 1.

Listen to each word that is read to you. Write the words on the lines provided.

1. ____________ 4. ____________ 7. ____________

2. ____________ 5. ____________ 8. ____________

3. ____________ 6. ____________ 9. ____________

Part 2.

Read the words below. In each word, underline the letter or letters that make the long *o* sound.

10. over

11. below

12. slope

13. grow

14. boat

15. note

16. foe

17. hello

18. toe

Name:

Long *o* and Sight Words

Part 3.

Choose the word from the box that best completes each sentence. Write the words on the lines provided.

against	come	neighbor	there
about	every	once	behind

19. I went to the shop ________________ today, not twice.

20. John hid ________________ that tree.

21. Please lean the bat ________________ the wall.

22. My ________________ is a very nice person.

23. It is time for Mark to ________________ home.

24. All the kids are waiting over ________________ .

25. I have ________________ five dollars in my pocket.

26. I like ________________ kind of candy.

Assessment

Name:

Long *o* and Sight Words

Part 4.

Write each word from the box in the correct column below according to its spelling of the long *o* sound.

blow	go	over	stone
float	foe	low	hello
toad	moat	doe	slow
no	note	lone	toe

27. ***o***

______

______

______

______

28. ***oa***

______

______

______

______

29. ***oe***

______

______

______

______

30. ***ow***

______

______

______

______

31. ***o*-consonant-*e***

______

______

______

______

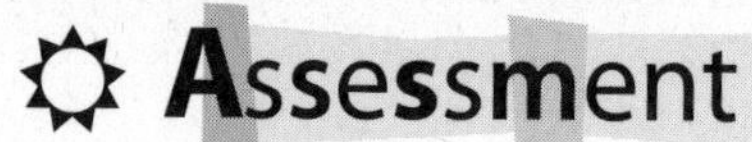

Name:

Long *o* and Sight Words

Part 5.

In each row, underline the word that is read to you.

32.	there	then	that
33.	again	gain	against
34.	now	new	no
35.	very	every	ever
36.	nested	shoulder	neighbor
37.	below	behind	because
38.	once	one	just
39.	came	come	core
40.	about	above	around

Name:

Long *e* and Sight Words 1

Practice Long *e*

Read each sentence aloud. Underline the word or words in each sentence that contain the long *e* sound. Then read each sentence again.

1. He told me his feet hurt.
2. I like to sleep late on the weekends.
3. Dad asked me to sweep the kitchen.
4. We had a picnic on the soft green grass.
5. Grandpa planted seeds in his garden.
6. Three birds sat chirping on the same tree branch.
7. She does not like when weeds grow next to her flowers.
8. The queen gave a speech.
9. Can we hike up that steep mountain?
10. We will meet under the tree across the street.

Name:

Long *e* and Sight Words 1

Complete the Sentences

Choose the word from the box that best completes each sentence. Write each word on the lines provided. Then read each sentence aloud.
Hint: One word will be used in two sentences.

about	behind	follow
neighbor	please	saw

1. James ________________ Kristin and waved.
2. The book fell ________________ the bookshelf.
3. Lane told Carl ________________ her track meet.
4. Our ________________ washes his car every weekend.
5. I always say "________________" when I ask for something.
6. My little brother likes to ________________ me everywhere I go.
7. The play was ________________ a boy who meets a dog that can talk.

Long *e* and Sight Words 1

Get Ready

- A *noun* is a word that names a person, place, thing, or idea. A *pronoun* is a word that takes the place of a noun. The prefix *pro-* in *pronoun* means "instead of" or "for." A pronoun can be used instead of, or for, a noun in a sentence.

- A *singular noun* names one person, place, thing, or idea. A *singular personal pronoun* replaces a singular proper or common noun in a sentence. The singular personal pronouns are *I*, *you*, *he*, *she*, *it*, *me*, *him*, and *her*. For example:

  A *bug* bit *Ted*.

  It bit *him*.

  Annie hurled the *football* at Dad.

  She hurled *it* at *him*.

- A *plural noun* names more than one person, place, thing, or idea. A *plural personal pronoun* replaces a plural proper or common noun in a sentence. The plural personal pronouns are *we*, *you*, *they*, *us*, and *them*. For example:

  The *children* picked the *apples*.

  They picked *them*.

- Plural personal pronouns refer to more than one person, place, thing, or idea. For example:

  Kara and I are going to summer camp.

  We are going to summer camp.

Try It

Replace the underlined word or words in each sentence below with a singular personal pronoun or a plural personal pronoun. Write the pronouns on the lines provided.

Example: The wagon rolled down the hill.

It rolled down the hill.

1. Jennifer jumped for joy.

   ______ jumped for joy.

2. You will find a rake in the shed.

   You will find ______ in the shed.

3. Mr. and Mrs. Jones asked Francis and Phillip to sing.

   ______ asked ______ to sing.

4. Amber and I watched the horses prance around the ring.

   ______ watched ______ prance around the ring.

5. Please give the book to Fred.

   Please give ______ to ______.

6. Carlos and Mindy work at the animal shelter every weekend.

   ______ work at the animal shelter every weekend.

Name:

Practice Long *e*

Choose the word from the box that best completes each sentence. Write each word on the lines provided. Then read each sentence aloud.

beak	eat	feel	neat	stream	we	wheat

1. Bread can be made from ________________.

2. What did you ________________ for lunch?

3. The bird used its ________________ to peck for food.

4. I ________________ tired in the mornings if I do not get enough sleep.

5. The animals drank water from the ________________.

6. I keep my side of the room ________________, but my sister does not.

7. Patrick and I will play in the yard after ________________ rake the leaves.

Choose three words from the box above. On the lines provided below, write a sentence using each word. Then read each sentence aloud.

8. ____

____

9. ____

____

10. ____

____

Name:

Sight Words Scramble

Unscramble each sight word. Write the unscrambled words on the lines provided.

1. oofllw ____________ **2.** aeelps ____________ **3.** asw ____________

Choose the sight word from above that best completes each sentence below. Write the words on the lines provided. Then read each sentence aloud.

4. ____________ turn off the light when you leave the room.

5. We ____________ the bird dive into the water and catch a fish.

6. If you ____________ the directions, you will not get lost.

On the lines provided, write a sentence using each sight word from above.

7. ____

____

8. ____

____

9. ____

____

sleeping bag sat up. "Good morning!" he said as he brushed the snow off his bag. Dean stared at the man in shock. "I hope I didn't scare you just now," he said. "I got stuck hiking up the mountain after dark last night. I saw your fire and thought it would be best to camp near your tent. My name is Brad, by the way." Dean leaned forward to shake his hand. "Mind if I hike down with you? It's easy to get lost in the snow. It hides the trail. I used to be a park ranger." With that, Joan and Dean said they would be more than happy to have Brad come with them. And whenever Joan and Dean told this story to their friends, they started with the line, "Let me tell you about the time we met a *real* snowman!"

The Snowman

Thump! Joan sat up with a jolt. "What was that?" she whispered to Dean. "Did you hear that?" Joan poked at what she thought was her brother's arm inside of his sleeping bag. *Thump*! "There it is again!" Joan said. "Dean, wake up!" Now she shook her brother hard. Dean rolled over to face Joan.

"What do you want?" Dean groaned. He sounded upset. "I was having the best dream." *Thump*! Dean sat up, too. Joan

leaned over to zip open the flap in the tent window. She peeked outside. "Is it a bear?" Dean asked. He was a little afraid.

"Oh, no!" shouted Joan. "It's snowing!" Joan watched as snowflakes drifted down from the dark, morning sky.

picked up anything they left behind. He kicked at the lumps of snow with the toe of his boot to be sure trash or gear wasn't hiding under it. Dean kicked at what looked like a small log.

"Ouch!" someone yelled. Dean jumped back. Something under the snow began to move. A man in a toast! How long do you think it will take us to hike down?" she asked as she opened a bag of fruit. It took them two days to walk up the steep slope. Joan bit into a red apple.

"It shouldn't take much time at all. It always goes faster when you're heading downhill," Dean said with his mouth full. "And we have less to pack. Not as much food and water to carry. I just hope we don't get lost in the snow." Dean poured more cereal into his bowl. "Camping sure makes me hungry!" he said. Once Dean had enough to eat, he left the tent. Next, he went over to the fire pit to make sure that last night's fire was really out. The pit was covered with snow. He stepped all over it just to make sure there were no embers left burning. The last thing he did was walk around the camp. He

"It must have snowed all night long. There's about two feet of the stuff out there," she said as she closed the flap.

"So, what's making that thumping sound?" asked Dean. "Snow is silent when it falls." Joan opened the flap again and poked her head out of the tent window. She looked all around. *Thump*! She craned her neck around and up.

"Oh!" she said. "It's the trees. There's so much snow on the branches that it's falling off in clumps. It must be too heavy. Anyway, the clumps of snow are falling right on our tent. If we don't do something about it, we are going to be buried alive!" she joked. "We better pack up."

"Now?" asked Dean. "It's so early! I need more sleep," he protested as he pulled his sleeping bag over his head. "Besides, I wanted to stay at least another day. What's it doing snowing this late in the year anyway?" But he knew his sister was right. If the snow kept falling, their tent would cave in. And they didn't bring cold-weather clothes. So, Joan and Dean started to pack up their gear. After he finished rolling up his sleeping bag, Dean said, "I don't know about you, but I need some food before we start down the mountain." He sat on his rolled-up bag.

"I already packed the stove," said Joan. "You'll have to eat some cold cereal and milk."

"I hope the milk isn't frozen!" said Dean. Joan smiled at her brother. He ran outside the tent to get the milk and

toasted wheat that was stored in the food locker. The snow made a crunchy sound as he walked over it. He cleared out the locker while he was getting his breakfast. Then he rushed back to the tent. "Could you hand me a bowl?" Dean asked. He held out his hand as he sat back down. "I'm starving."

"Here you go," said Joan as she handed one to him. "Make it fast. I want to leave as soon as possible."

"You sound funny," Dean said. "Are you OK?" Dean stopped what he was doing to take a good look at his sister.

"My throat is sore," Joan replied. "That's why I sound a little hoarse. I sure hope I'm not getting sick." Joan rubbed her throat with worry. "I could use some hot tea and lemon. And some warm

Name:

Long *e* and Sight Words 3

Long *e*

Read aloud each word in the box. Then write each word from the box in the correct column below according to the spelling of the long *e* sound. Last, write one new word of your own in each column.

be	steam	yield	screech
least	free	brownie	beans
we	me	greet	shriek

e	*ee*	*ea*	*ie*

Choose one word from each column above. On the lines provided below, write a sentence using each word. Then read each sentence aloud.

1. ____________________

2. ____________________

3. ____________________

4. ____________________

Name:

Long *e* and Sight Words 3

Complete the Sentences

Choose the word from the box that best completes each sentence. Write each word on the lines provided. Then read each sentence aloud.
Hint: One word will be used in two sentences.

everything	about	please
saw	under	whether

1. The dog slept ______________ the chair.
2. Joan and I ______________ that movie last week.
3. We sat in the shade ______________ the big tree.
4. Will you ______________ help me move the table?
5. I packed ______________ I needed for my trip to the beach.
6. Mom told me ______________ the things she liked to do when she was my age.
7. Lauren had to decide ______________ to keep the stuffed animal or give it to her sister.

Name:

Practice Long *e*

Choose the word from the box that best completes each sentence. Write each word on the lines provided. Then underline the letters that make the long *e* sound in each word. The first one has been done for you.

athletes	bleed	brief	clean	he
here	me	thief	weak	weep

1. The opposite of she is he.
2. Another word for cry is __________.
3. The opposite of strong is __________.
4. You __________ something that is dirty.
5. If you cut yourself you might __________.
6. People who play sports are __________.
7. If something is short or quick it is __________.
8. Someone who steals from others is a __________.
9. Something that is in this place is __________.
10. A word you use when you are talking about yourself is __________.

Name:

Long *e* and Sight Words 4

By Sight

See how many words you can read correctly in one minute. Read aloud across the rows. When you get to the bottom of the page, start over. Try to read more words the second time.

about	baby	come	everything	follow
held	love	many	neighbor	once
please	saw	there	under	very
whether	above	behind	could	every
here	more	none	other	people
should	together	while	against	brother
move	now	sister	would	animals

Number of words read correctly: ______

to feed the dog. After I fed Sandy, I got my fishing pole. Then Sandy and I walked down to the creek. While I was there, I slipped and fell into the water. I started to get washed downstream! Sandy began to bark and run up and down the side of the creek. I had to fight the rushing water. It took me forever to get back to shore. I felt so weak! I had to sit down to catch my breath. Then I couldn't find my fishing pole. Oh, well!

When I felt better, we walked slowly back to the house. All I wanted to do was to get into a dry T-shirt and a pair of shorts. Lucky for me everyone was gone when we got home. Now I could take a nap. What a weekend. I need some sleep!

What a Weekend

What a weekend! It seems like I had something to do every minute. It started early Saturday morning. Mom said I had to clean my room. "Not just tidy it up," she said. "*Clean* it." I had to go through everything. That's how I found an old piece of strawberry cheesecake. It was under my bed. It was covered with green, hairy fuzz. Mom was not pleased! I also found a bag of jellybeans beneath some papers on my teak desk. And then I found

a candy bar deep inside my tweed coat pocket. I sure like my sweet treats!

By the time I finished cleaning, there was a big pile of dirty socks and jeans on the rug. So I had to do the wash. Then it was time for my regular chores.

were gone. Good, because I had to go back out there and sweep up the grass clippings! And I had to plant some green beans and beets. Mom had asked me to do that yesterday.

I got the seed packets and went to work. The soil was still pretty muddy from the rain. That made it easier to pull some weeds. While I was in the garden, I could hear something honking up above me. It was a flock of geese flying back home. They go south every winter. It was good to see them. It means spring is really here. I know they couldn't see me, but I waved "hello" to them. It filled me with glee.

When I was done, I went inside to wash up. Dad was just about to leave to go play golf. He said it was my turn me. I had to flee into the house. I counted three welts. One was on my hand. One was on my cheek. The last one was on my ear, of all places! Lucky for me that's all I got. But I have to admit, the pain made me shed a tear or two.

After about an hour, Dad went outside to see if the coast was clear. The bees

I didn't have to water the garden or mow the lawn because it was raining. But I did have to take out the trash. That shouldn't be a big deal. But I had to put on all my rain gear. I hate those rain boots! They squeak when I walk. Plus, my raincoat is too shiny. I think I look silly. I put about a ream of paper in the paper bin. Then I put a bunch of jars in the glass bin. Then I dumped a bucket of scraps, like orange peels, in the compost bin. My family throws away very little. "Reduce, reuse, recycle." That's what Dad likes to say.

When I was through with my chores, I thought I would play a game on my computer. Nope! Dad said he needed me to help him fix the furnace. It wasn't making any heat. By the time we were done it was time for lunch. We both had a big bowl of split pea soup. Yum! After lunch, I checked outside. The rain was gone and it was sunny now. So I went to the park to meet my pal, Mary. We're on a field hockey team. We wanted to run some drills. I can't tell you how many times I ran up and down that field! It made me really hungry. Lucky I had some peanuts in my sports bag. When I got home, I wanted to relax and read. But Lee, my sister, wanted to have a tea party. So we sat around a small table with her dolls. I put pretend cream in my pretend tea. We ate candy and nuts out of little paper cups. We had a dandy time!

When it was time for dinner, Mom asked Dad and me to pick up a pizza. Just before we got to the pizza shop, a car pulled out in front of us. Dad hit the horn so hard it cracked the steering

wheel. Dad was steamed! After we ate, we watched our favorite TV shows.

Later that night, it started to rain again. But this time the wind kicked up. It howled and howled. We had to keep the radio on all night to hear if a tornado was coming. I don't think any of us got any sleep.

I was pretty tired Sunday morning. At least the storm was over. Now I had a chance to mow the lawn. It was a good day for mowing—not too hot, with a nice breeze. I was shocked when I went outside. I think the rain made the grass grow three inches overnight! I got out the mower and started in the backyard. It was going fine until I went by the old cherry tree. I don't know what happened. All of a sudden, a swarm of bees came at me. *Help*! I could feel a few of them sting

Name:

Unit 16 Assessment

Part 1.

Read each word below. On the lines provided, write *Y* for *yes* if the word contains the long *e* sound. Write *N* for *no* if the word does not contain the long *e* sound.

1. be ____
2. needs ____
3. held ____
4. chief ____
5. heat ____
6. pressed ____
7. extreme ____
8. queen ____
9. fresh ____
10. dreams ____

Part 2.

Listen to each word that is read to you. Write each word on the lines provided.

11. ____________
12. ____________
13. ____________
14. ____________
15. ____________
16. ____________
17. ____________
18. ____________
19. ____________
20. ____________

☼ Assessment

Name:

Long *e* and Sight Words

Part 3.

In each row, underline the word that contains the long *e* sound.

21.	me	melt	men
22.	felt	feet	fed
23.	beads	belt	best
24.	field	filled	fled
25.	hens	helped	here
26.	tame	team	them
27.	wet	weld	weep
28.	yes	yield	yet
29.	day	dented	deal
30.	we	west	well

Name:

Long *e* and Sight Words

Part 4.

In each row, underline the word that is read to you.

31.	about	animals	almost
32.	everything	every	even
33.	father	follow	friend
34.	nothing	none	next
35.	out	only	over
36.	put	pull	please
37.	sister	saw	some
38.	under	unless	until
39.	while	whether	walk
40.	north	napkin	nothing
41.	once	over	other
42.	almost	above	against

Name:

Long *e* and Sight Words

Part 5.

Read each word aloud.

43. over

44. nothing

45. almost

46. whether

47. under

48. saw

49. please

50. over

51. nothing

52. follow

53. everything

54. almost

Name:

Get Ready

Personal Pronouns as Subjects of Sentences

The **subject** of a sentence tells who or what the sentence is about. What is the subject of the following sentence?

The astronaut blasted off in the rocket.

To find the subject, ask, "Who or what is the sentence about?" Who or what blasted off in the rocket? *The astronaut* is the subject of the sentence. You can replace *the astronaut* with a pronoun, but only certain **personal pronouns** should be used as the subjects of a sentence. These are:

singular:	I	you	he	she	it
plural:	we	you	they		

So, you could say:

She blasted off in the rocket. OR *He* blasted off in the rocket.

Personal Pronouns After Verbs

Find the verb in this sentence:

The artists draw their sketches on the walls.

The verb is *draw*. What do the artists draw on the walls? Their sketches. You can replace *their sketches* with a pronoun, but in most cases, only certain personal pronouns are used *after the verb* in a sentence. They are sometimes called **object pronouns**. These pronouns are:

singular:	me	you	him	her	it
plural:	us	you	them		

So, you could say:

The artists draw *them* on the walls.

Name:

Long *e* and Sight Words 5

Try It

Underline the subject pronoun in each sentence.

1. We read books to learn about the moon.
2. It has craters.
3. They are really deep holes in the moon's surface.
4. Someday, I would like to visit the moon.

Try It

Underline the correct pronoun in parentheses that completes each sentence.

5. That mean hornet chased (I, me)!
6. We have never met (he, him) before.
7. My father says he has seen (them, they).
8. Andrew is driving into town with (her, she).
9. Kevin and (me, I) would like to write a book together.
10. (Her, She) and Rose will travel together this summer.
11. The governor asked (us, we) to sing at the ceremony.

Name:

Long *e* Spelled *ie* and Sight Words

Long *e* Practice

Read each word below aloud. Then draw a line to connect the words that rhyme.

brief	yield
shield	piece
niece	chief

Choose the word from the box that best completes each sentence. Write the words on the lines provided. Then read each sentence aloud.

piece	believe	brief	thief	niece	field

1. Chuck ate a ________________ of cake for a snack.
2. "A ________________ stole my gold watch!" shouted Will.
3. Greg's ________________ is ten years old.
4. Let's play a game of tag in the ________________ .
5. "I ________________ that I will win the race," Eve said.
6. The TV did not work for a ________________ time today.

Name:

Long *e* Spelled *ie* and Sight Words

Missing Letters

Underline the letter in parentheses that completes each word. Write the completed word on the line provided. Then say the word aloud.

1. th_re (a, u, e) ________
2. o_er (f, v, w) ________
3. plea_e (z, s, c) ________
4. _gainst (a, o, e) ________
5. alm_st (e, o, a) ________
6. u_der (n, m, l) ________
7. no_ (h, v, w) ________
8. n_thing (e, o, a) ________
9. und_r (e, i, o) ________
10. sa_ (r, v, w) ________

by Mom's face that there was no point in trying to get her to yield. And, to tell you the truth, it was a bit of a relief. No sports for a week. This is going to be a first! What would I do with all that free time?

Time Out!

My family is big on sports. My oldest brother, Sam, plays on an ice hockey team. Last year, his team won the state finals. My other brother, Rex, is a jockey. That means he trains and rides horses for a living. My sister, Meg, plays softball. She's the main pitcher on her team. She is a key player on the local field hockey squad, too. My dad has made a lot of

We were pleased to find out that each one of us had a free week in late May. It would be a great time to drive up to Cold Caves, too, because the weather would be just right—not too hot and not too cold. And all the spring flowers would be popping up by then. Mom would like that.

“I am really thrilled about this, Dear,” Dad said to Mom as he gave her a big hug. “I think I'll start packing right now. I'm going to shine up my spare bag of golf clubs and put them in the van right after I have lunch.”

“No!” Mom shouted. “No balls, no clubs, no pucks, no nothing! This will be a sports-free trip!” Once again we all stared at each other. We could tell and stared at each other for what felt like an hour. No one said a word.

"You know," Meg said at last, "I have wanted to see Cold Caves since I was a kid."

"So have I!" Sam said.

"Me too!" Rex said.

"I haven't been there since I was a small boy!" Dad said.

"I would love to see Cold Caves!" I said.

"That settles it!" Mom said with joy. "Cold Caves it is! Now comes the hard part. What week can we all take off?" By now we were all keen on making it work. We all went over our plans.

money over the years playing golf. He used to be a chief player. Now he's the golf pro at the local sports club. In fact, I'm his caddy when he plays at events. Dad says that's a fine way for me to learn the game. Then there's my mother. Mom used to be a surfing pro. She traveled to lots of beach towns all over the globe when she was a teenager so she could be in surfing contests. She's a nurse now, but she still surfs on weekends. Last, but not least, there's me, Todd. I am on a basketball team and a baseball team, and I speed skate on ice in the winter. Like I said, my family is big on sports!

And that's the problem. My family spends so much time playing sports that we almost never see each other. The only time I see my dad is when I caddy for him. My brothers, sister, and I only see each other when we pass in the hall. I can't think of the last time all six of us sat down and had a meal together. Mom says this is a bad thing. So, today she called a family meeting. I was sure she was going to give us grief about it again.

"I have had it!" Mom shrieked. "We are taking a family trip! We need to spend some time together, just the six of us. Let's pick a time and a place to go right now!" Mom slammed her hand down on the table. We all looked at her in shock.

"But I have games planned!" Sam said.

"And I have my job at the club!" Dad said.

"And I have to train horses!" Rex said.

"And I have games planned, too!" I said.

"So do I!" Meg said.

Mom got up and glared at us. Her hands were clenched in fists. "You will not get me to believe that you all can't find one week out of the year to spend time with your family," she said. "I tell you, I am not getting out of this chair until we plan our trip!" She sat back down with a pout and crossed her arms over her chest. Mom was mad! We sat

Name:

Long *e* Spelled *ey*

Read the clues to fill in the crossword puzzle with words from the box.
Hint: Not every word in the word box is used.

honey	jersey	key	jockey	monkey
donkey	valley	turkey	money	kidney

Across

1. an animal that lives in a rainforest
2. this is used to buy things
3. this is used to unlock a door

Down

4. an animal that can be used to pull a cart
5. this kind of shirt is worn when playing football or soccer
6. bees make this sweet stuff

					4			5	
				1					
		6							
	2								
3									

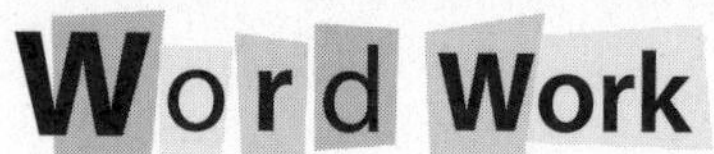

Name:

Long *e* Spelled *ey* and Sight Words

Sight Word Jumble

Read aloud each sight word in the box.

follow	number	whether
under	write	over
please	children	nothing

Now find and circle each sight word in the jumble below.
Hint: There is one sight word in each row of letters.

n	u	m	b	e	r	y	l
s	n	o	t	h	i	n	g
t	r	o	v	e	r	m	d
w	h	e	t	h	e	r	n
c	h	i	l	d	r	e	n
w	r	i	t	e	o	t	v
v	e	p	l	e	a	s	e
f	o	l	l	o	w	e	b
p	u	t	u	n	d	e	r

Long *e* Spelled *ey* and Sight Words

Get Ready

Possessive Pronouns

If you possess something, you own it. Possessive nouns show ownership or relationship.

Possessive pronouns show possession by telling *who owns something*.

Study this chart of possessive pronouns.

Pronoun	Ownership	Example
mine	belonging to me	The red hat is **mine**.
ours	belonging to us	That house is **ours**.
yours	belonging to you	This cap is **yours**.
his	belonging to him	He lost **his** last night.
hers	belonging to her	Annie found **hers** at school.
theirs	belonging to them	Please bring **theirs** to them.

Try It

Underline the possessive pronoun in each sentence.
Hint: One sentence has two possessive pronouns.

1. That car looks like ours.
2. Mine was over here unless someone moved it.
3. Is that dog theirs?
4. Hers is more colorful than his.
5. Where did you put yours?

Name:

Long *e* Spelled *y* and Sight Words

Long *e*

Read aloud each word in the box. Underline each word that contains the long *e* sound.

cake	many	break
happy	crest	gem
anything	speck	ladybug
heard	story	stretch
feather	babysit	city
pretty	chestnut	jellyfish

Choose three of the words with the long *e* sound from the box above. On the lines provided below, write each word in a sentence.

1. ______________________________

2. ______________________________

3. ______________________________

Choose the Sight Word

Find a word in the word box that has a similar meaning to the underlined word or words in each sentence. Write the word from the box on the line provided. An example has been done for you.

number	over	children	everything
nothing	almost	write	under

Example: The kids walked to the park.

children

1. There was not anything that I could do to help.

____

2. You need to print your name on this form.

____

3. The cat hid below the bed.

____

4. A bunch of dogs at the animal shelter have black fur.

____

5. There are about one hundred people at the fair.

____

6. The bird soared above the trees.

____

7. The fire burned all of it.

____

the team looked glum and walked away with their heads down. But Hal could not stop smiling. He was the happiest he had ever been.

"Thanks, guys!" Hal said as the team gathered around him. "I mean girls!" Everyone laughed. Hal was going to fit right in.

Field Hockey Hal

Hal is a boy who loves to run. And because Hal loves to run, he also loves to play field hockey. You need to run a lot to play this game.

Hal is new in town. His family just moved to Pier City last month. Yesterday, Hal saw an ad in the newspaper for the local field hockey team. They needed one new player. Tryouts would be held this Saturday. Hal was excited. He really wanted to be on the team. It would be

a good way to meet local kids, too. Any team would be lucky to have me, Hal thought to himself. No one can wield a hockey stick like me! But just one new player. This might be tough. So, Hal practiced all Friday afternoon to make sure he would be at his best.

"OK, girls," Coach said as she passed out slips of paper to each team member. "Write the name of the person you want to join the team on this piece of paper. Fold it in half and then put it in the can." Coach pointed to an empty coffee can. "I'll add up all the votes. The player with the highest number of votes will be our new team member." The girls did what Coach said. Then she counted the votes. "I can't believe this," said Coach as she scratched her head. "This is a first. Everyone voted for the same player!" Hal held his breath. He could feel his heart beating in his chest again. This is it, he thought. The moment of truth. "The new player for the Pier City Field Hockey Team is... Hal!" shouted Coach. All the girls on the team let out a shriek of joy. All the new girls who tried out for his stick, which isn't easy to do. Hal was so into the game that he didn't hear the girls on the sideline cheering him on. "Go, Hal!" they cried. All Hal wanted to do was score.

Just before Hal got to the goal, another player charged at him. Hal passed the ball to the girl on his left. She ran the ball around another player. Then she passed the ball back to Hal. Now Hal was right in front of the goal. He hit the ball hard. He could feel his heart beating in his chest. Would the ball make it? All the girls yelled at once. "SCORE!" Just then, Coach blew the whistle. The practice game was over. Hal ran back to join the group. Some of the girls patted him on the back. He heard more than one girl tell him he did a great job. Hal took it as a good sign.

Hal got up early Saturday morning. He wanted to be sure he wasn't late for tryouts. Hal checked his gear. Shoes with cleats? Check! Shin guards? Check! Knee socks? Check! Safety goggles? Gloves? Check and check! Hal put everything on. Then he grabbed his stick and was ready to go.

When Hal got to the park, all he saw were girls. The same thing happened back home. The team was all girls. They wouldn't let Hal play with them. He and the guys had to start their own team. I sure hope they let me play, Hal thought to himself. I don't know anybody here. I don't think I could start a team even if I wanted to!

Coach had all the children who were at the park for tryouts line up. They had to put on name tags. Then Coach introduced everyone to the girls on the field hockey team. Coach had the new kids do some exercises to warm up. When they were done with that, she had them run some drills. First she had the kids practice passing the ball to each other. Next she had them run down the field to show how well they could control the ball. The last thing she had them do was take turns hitting the ball into the goal. Coach and the team members took notes the whole time.

When the kids finished the drills, Coach split them into two practice teams. Hal was put on the team with the green jerseys. The girls on his team were all talking to each other. But no one talked to Hal. That's OK, Hal thought to himself. I'll just have to show them what

a great player I am. Then they will all want to talk to me.

Coach blew the whistle. The practice game was on! For the longest time, Hal just ran up and down the field. No one would pass the ball to him. Then a player on the other team made a bad pass. Hal jumped at the chance to show his stuff. He stole the ball and ran down the field. The same player came running after him. She tried to steal the ball back. Hal ran around her so fast she didn't even see him. Another player came at him. Hal used his skills and avoided her, too. Then another player ran straight for Hal. For a brief moment he thought she might get the ball away from him. But Hal got away from her and kept going. All the while, he kept the ball close to

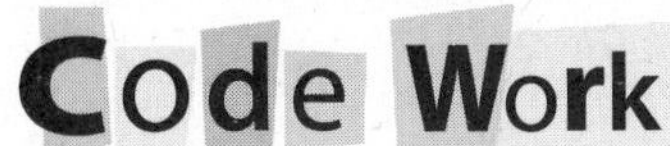

Name:

Long *i*

Read each sentence aloud. In each sentence, underline the word that contains the long *i* sound.

1. Rick wondered why Betty was late for dinner.
2. "Your baby brother is so shy!" Randy said to Kay.
3. We plan to take a trip to Quail City in July.
4. "I would rather go to the fair myself," Gail said.
5. Help me put these wet shirts in the dryer.
6. Jill watched the pretty bird fly to its little nest.

Read the word at the beginning of each line. On the lines provided, write a sentence using the word.

7. cry ______________________________
____
8. try ______________________________
____
9. my ______________________________
____
10. sky ______________________________
____

Sight Word Recognition

Underline the sight word listed as many times as it appears in each row.

1. its	it	sits	its	is	its
2. nothing	nothing	noting	netting	nothing	noting
3. under	under	udder	under	until	udder
4. first	fist	first	firs	fist	first
5. write	white	wife	write	write	white
6. because	became	because	beacons	because	beacons
7. number	number	mumble	rubber	number	mumble
8. almost	almost	almost	almonds	almanac	almond
9. children	chilled	chiller	children	chilled	children

Choose three sight words from the list above. On the lines provided, write each word in a sentence.

10. ______________________________

____

11. ______________________________

____

12. ______________________________

____

Name:

Unit 17 Assessment

Part 1.

Listen to each word that is read to you. Write each word on the lines provided.

1. ____________________
2. ____________________
3. ____________________
4. ____________________
5. ____________________
6. ____________________
7. ____________________
8. ____________________

Part 2.

Read each word below. On the lines provided, write *Y* for *yes* if the word contains the long *e* sound. Write *N* for *no* if the word does not contain the long *e* sound.

9. stretch ______
10. kidney ______
11. jersey ______
12. jelly ______
13. dresses ______
14. heard ______

☼ Assessment

Name:

Long *e* & Long *i* and Sight Words

Part 3.

Read each word below. On the lines provided, write *Y* for *yes* if the word contains the long *i* sound. Write *N* for *no* if the word does not contain the long *i* sound.

15. hitch ______

16. hockey ______

17. skylark ______

18. frying ______

19. baby ______

20. shy ______

Part 4.

Write each word from the box in the correct column below according to the spelling of the long *e* sound.

key	chief	valley	happy	field
baby	money	niece	hockey	funny

21. ***ie***	**22.** ***ey***	**23.** ***y***

Name:

Part 5.

Write each word from the box in the correct column below according to the sound the *y* makes.

sky	city	many	dryer
myself	puppy	ladybug	shy

24. long *i*	25. long *e*

Name:

Long *e* & Long *i* and Sight Words

Part 5.

In each row, underline the word that is read to you.

26.	chilled	children	child
27.	evening	everyone	everything
28.	almost	amongst	amiss
29.	where	winter	whether
30.	ride	write	white
31.	first	fern	fist
32.	is	its	it
33.	nothing	noting	mother
34.	amber	nimble	number
35.	under	udder	amber
36.	of	oven	over
37.	begins	because	before

Name:

Long *u* and Closed Syllables 1

Practice Long *u*

Read each sentence aloud. Underline the word or words in each sentence that contain the long *u* sound. Then read each sentence again.

1. I added ice cubes to my tea.
2. Julie's new kitten is very cute.
3. We could see fumes coming out of the old car's tailpipe.
4. Mules are used to carry and pull heavy loads.
5. Chris put the television on mute.
6. We only have a few minutes until the concert starts!
7. My mom's nephew is my cousin.
8. We plugged too many things in to the light socket and blew a fuse.
9. The bugle is very loud!
10. I had a huge ice cream cone after lunch.

Long *u* and Closed Syllables 1

By Sight

See how many words you can read correctly in one minute. Read aloud across the rows. When you get to the bottom of the page, start over. Try to read more words the second time.

about	baby	children	everything	first
here	its	many	neighbor	once
please	saw	these	whether	above
because	come	follow	move	nothing
other	people	should	together	under
while	against	behind	now	over
write	almost	number	animals	none

Number of words read correctly: ______

Get Ready

Adverbs That Tell *When*

Adverbs tell more about verbs. An adverb can tell *when* an action is happening. For example:

The stray cat howled *late* in the night.

Verb: howled

Adverb: late (tells *when* the stray cat howled in the night)

Here are some common adverbs that tell *when*. These are not all of the adverbs that tell when, just some of the ones that we use often.

now	then	later	always	never	sometimes
before	soon	finally	yesterday	today	tomorrow

Adverbs That Tell *Where*

Some adverbs tell *where* an action takes place. For example:

Lily plays with sand *outside*.

Here are some adverbs that tell *where*:

up	down	inside	outside
nearby	far	there	here

Adverbs That Tell *How*

Some adverbs tell *how* an action takes place. For example:

Carl laughed *loudly* and *joyously*.

Many, but not all, adverbs that tell how end in *–ly*. Here are some adverbs that tell *how*:

quickly	slowly	happily	sadly
quietly	loudly	safely	softly

Name:

Try It – When, Where, and How

In these sentences, the verbs are circled. Underline the adverbs.
Hint: One sentence will have more than one kind of adverb.

1. It is hard to run backward.
2. The baby slept peacefully.
3. I left my book outside yesterday.
4. Clint walked upstairs to his room.
5. The opera singer sang beautifully.
6. Susie plays at my house sometimes.
7. I looked closely at the fish in the tank.
8. Yesterday I picked a basket of peaches.
9. Jennifer kicked the winning goal again.
10. The birds always fly south in the winter.
11. We ran outside to watch the fireworks.
12. The crowd cheered wildly for the team.
13. Please move the light away from my eyes.
14. My mother whispered softly to my little brother.
15. The families on our street are planning a party soon.

Name:

Long *u* and Closed Syllables 2

Practice Long *u*

Choose the word from the box that best completes each sentence. Write each word on the lines provided. Then read each sentence aloud.

cute	fumes	huge	mule	nephew

1. Most people think puppies are ________________.
2. The ________________ from that old car smell awful!
3. The hikers climbed the ________________ mountain.
4. A donkey looks a lot like a ________________.
5. Blake is my sister's son, so he is my ________________.

Choose two words from the box above. On the lines provided below, write a sentence using each word. Then read each sentence aloud.

6. ____

____

7. ____

____

8. ____

____

Name:

Long *u* and Closed Syllables 2

Closed Syllables

Underline the closed syllable in each word.
Hint: Some words have more than one closed syllable.

1. pretend
2. thunder
3. respect
4. moment
5. problem
6. platter
7. ponder
8. apple
9. sudden
10. relish

and walked back to the blanket. Now they could start their picnic. They ate many treats. When they were done, the girls went back to exploring the yard.

Ty had just finished cleaning up when his mom came outside. "So, how did it go?" she asked. "Did you have any trouble?"

"Someday, I'll tell you the whole story," Ty said as he began to walk into the house. "But I'll tell you three things right now. One, you were right. Two, you need to give the babysitter a raise. And three, I need a nap!" And with that, Ty put down the basket and the blanket. Then he plopped himself onto the sofa and fell fast asleep. Babysitting triplets is hard work!

Triple Trouble

Ty has three little sisters. His sisters were all born on the same day. That's right! Ty's little sisters are triplets! Their names are Bonnie, Josie, and Molly. But everybody just calls them Bo, Jo, and Mo.

One day in July, Ty's mother needed to drive into the city to buy a pair of shoes. The regular babysitter couldn't come. So Mom asked Ty if he would look after his sisters while she was gone.

"No problem!" Ty said. "In fact, I think I'll take the girls to the park for a picnic." Ty's mother let out a gasp.

"You want to take your three sisters to the park?" his mother asked. "All by yourself? Are you serious?"

That's when Ty got smart! He took Jo with him to find Bo. When they found her, he took both Bo and Jo to find Mo. Mo was trying to open the back gate. Lucky it was locked! Now he had all three girls together. They all held hands and ran around the yard. Somehow, Ty chased her over to the blanket. But when they got there, Bo was gone.

"Jo, where did Bo go?" he asked. Jo pointed to the dog house. Ty looked over and saw that Bo was playing with the new puppy. He ran to get Bo. But Bo didn't want to leave the puppy and started to cry. Ty had to pick her up and carry her to the blanket. But when he got there, Jo was gone.

"Where is Jo?" he asked Mo. Mo just held up her doll and said, "Pretty!" Ty ran around the yard until he found Jo. She was playing with some ants by the side of the house. Ty picked the ants off of her. Then he took her by the hand and they walked back to the blanket. This time, both Bo and Mo were gone.

"Sure. What's the big deal?" asked Ty. "They're just little girls. We can walk to the park. We'll have a nice lunch outside. And then they can play while I read a book." Ty smiled. "It will be fun!"

"I'm not sure that's such a good idea," said Ty's mother. She didn't look very happy. "Why not have this picnic of yours in our own backyard? That way the girls can't run too far. You know how they love to run and explore." Ty stared at his mother. He didn't understand.

"I don't know what you think is going to happen," Ty said. "I can take care of them by myself! But, OK, we'll have our picnic out back instead of at the park." Ty's mother let out a sigh of relief. She kissed the girls goodbye and told them to obey their big brother. The girls just giggled and ran into their room.

"Good luck, sweetie," she said to Ty as she got in the car. "Call me if you need to." Ty just smiled, nodded his head, and waved goodbye. He went into the kitchen to put together a picnic basket. Then he found an old blanket to sit on. When everything was all set up in the yard, he called to the girls and told them it was time for a picnic. Bo, Jo, and Mo came pouring out of their room and ran right outside. Ty thought they would run to the blanket he had set up. Instead, each girl ran to a different part of the yard. Bo ran over to the garden. Jo ran over to the sandbox. And Mo ran over to the swings.

"No, girls! Come over to the blanket!" Ty yelled to his sisters. "We're going to have a picnic!" But the girls were too busy

exploring and didn't hear him. So Ty went to round them up. First he rushed over to the garden to get Bo. She was playing in the dirt and was all muddy.

"Ladybug!" Bo shouted as she pointed to a flower. Ty nodded as he washed her hands off with the hose. Then they headed back to the blanket. Ty gave her a napkin to dry herself off. He told Bo to stay put as he went and got her two sisters. Next Ty went over to the sandbox to get Jo. She was covered with sand. Ty brushed off her sandy shorts. Then he took Jo by the hand and led her back to the blanket. He gave her a towel to clean her hands. He told her to stay with Bo until he got back. Then he went to the swings. He told Mo she had to come eat lunch. But Mo jumped off her swing

Practice Long *u* Spellings

Choose the words from the box that best match each clue. Write each word on the lines provided. Then underline the letters that make the long *u* sound in each word. An example has been done for you.

argue	curfew	fuel	huge
menu	nephew	rescue	humid

Example: Another word for save is rescue.

1. Something that is very large is ________.
2. Coal, wood, oil, and gas are kinds of ________.
3. It is ________ when the air is damp.
4. When people do not agree, they may ________.
5. The son of your brother or sister would be your ________.
6. A ________ is a set time a person must be home at night.
7. You look at a ________ to find out what a restaurant serves.

Name:

Long *u* and Closed Syllables 3

Closed Syllables

Draw a line from the syllable on the left to a syllable on the right to make a word. Write the word on the line provided below. Then read each word aloud. The first one has been done for you.

1.	bas	pet
2.	pup	nic
3.	nap	ket
4.	pic	box
5.	sand	kin
6.	ten	shell
7.	cob	bit
8.	nut	nis
9.	cac	web
10.	rab	tus

11. basket ____________ **16.** ____________

12. ____________ **17.** ____________

13. ____________ **18.** ____________

14. ____________ **19.** ____________

15. ____________ **20.** ____________

Name:

Unit 18 Assessment

Part 1.

Read each word below. On the lines provided, write *Y* for *yes* if the word contains the long *u* sound. Write *N* for *no* if the word does not contain the long *u* sound.

1. menu ______
2. dusted ______
3. found ______
4. fuse ______
5. rescue ______
6. pulled ______
7. curfew ______
8. used ______
9. would ______
10. pupil ______

Part 2.

Listen to each word that is read to you. Write each word on the lines provided.

11. ____________
12. ____________
13. ____________
14. ____________
15. ____________

Name:

Long *u* and Syllable Types

Part 3.

In each row, underline the word that contains the long *u* sound.

16.	arched	argue	artful
17.	cube	curled	cups
18.	found	flush	fumes
19.	human	hounded	hurting
20.	mules	must	munch
21.	nephew	never	near
22.	vault	voice	value
23.	curb	cue	cut
24.	hunch	hug	humid
25.	mouth	music	mugs

Assessment

Name:

Long *u* and Syllable Types

Part 4.

On the lines provided, write the number of syllables that each word contains.

26. children ______

27. write ______

28. together ______

29. number ______

30. nothing ______

31. saw ______

32. almost ______

33. fantastic ______

34. over ______

35. animals ______

Part 5.

Listen to each word that is read to you. On the lines provided, write *Y* for *yes* if the word begins with a closed syllable. Write *N* for *no* if the word does not begin with a closed syllable.

36. ______

37. ______

38. ______

39. ______

40. ______

41. ______

42. ______

43. ______

44. ______

45. ______

Name:

Part 6.

Read each word. On the lines provided, write *Y* for *yes* if the word begins with a closed syllable. Write *N* for *no* if the word does not begin with a closed syllable.

46. cobweb ______

47. cactus ______

48. frozen ______

49. puppet ______

50. basic ______

51. lady ______

52. fabric ______

53. rabbit ______

54. motel ______

55. robot ______

Name:

/o͞o/ Word Scramble

Unscramble each word below. Write the unscrambled words on the lines provided. Then read each word aloud.
Hint: Each word contains the sound /o͞o/.

1. tufle ______________
2. ewd ______________
3. dreu ______________
4. nute ______________
5. wen ______________
6. urnpe ______________
7. whec ______________
8. elru ______________
9. wescr ______________
10. whert ______________

Choose two words from above. Write each word in a sentence on the lines provided below.

11. ____

____

12. ____

____

Name:

Break It Up!

Each word below contains two closed syllables. Read each word aloud. Draw a line between the two syllables in each word.

1. p u m p k i n
2. c h a p t e r
3. s u n s e t
4. i t s e l f
5. b a c k p a c k
6. r o b i n
7. c h i p m u n k
8. e x i t
9. r a b b i t
10. n u t s h e l l
11. c a b i n
12. i n s e c t
13. e n t e r

Get Ready

- An **adverb** can tell *when* an action is happening. For example: Pete went to the zoo *yesterday*. The adverb *yesterday* tells *when* Pete went to the zoo.

  Here are some common adverbs that tell *when*.

today	tomorrow	now	then
soon	finally	always	before
later	yesterday	sometimes	never

- An adverb can tell *where* an action is happening. For example: Jake is standing *outside*. The adverb *outside* tells *where* Jake is standing.

  Here are some common adverbs that tell *where*.

up	down	inside	outside
below	somewhere	nowhere	above
far	near	here	there

- An adverb can tell *how* an action is happening. For example: Martin laughed *loudly*. The adverb *loudly* tells *how* Martin laughed.

  Here are some common adverbs that tell *how*.

quickly	loudly	sadly	quietly
slowly	softly	safely	weakly
neatly	clearly	calmly	badly

Name:

Try It

In each sentence, underline the adverb that tells *when*.

1. Yesterday I ate some plums.
2. We always go to the last game of the season.
3. Sometimes Nick plays at my house.
4. The sun finally came out.

In each sentence, underline the adverb that tells *where*.

5. Ross looked up at the sky.
6. I know my books are somewhere!
7. Put the plate here.
8. We live near the lake.

In each sentence, underline the adverb that tells *how*.

9. Jill ran to the store quickly.
10. Sam spoke softly to me.
11. Tom went into the house quietly.
12. Please speak clearly into the phone.

Name:

Long Double *o* Spelled *ue*

Use the clues to complete the crossword puzzle. The answer to each clue is a word from the box.
Hint: Not every word in the box is used.

rule	chew	tuba	Sue	blue
truth	prune	glue	new	tuna

Across

1. this stuff is sticky
2. a dried plum
3. a kind of fish

Down

4. the opposite of a lie
5. the color of the sky
6. a girl's name
7. the opposite of old

						6
				5		
			1			
	4					
2						
	3		7			

Name:

Open Syllables

Say the words in the box aloud. Underline each word that begins with an open syllable.

exit	hotel	relax	insect
tulip	robin	robot	enter
until	begin	itself	secret

Use four of the words you underlined above to complete the following sentences below. Write each word on the lines provided.

1. The ______________ was closed for the winter.
2. I like to ______________ after working in the yard all day.
3. James forgot his ______________ password.
4. The ______________ is my favorite spring flower.

"June, you are my hero!" she shouted "You should have seen yourself! You looked like you really were a lifeguard!" Ava said as she jumped up and down and clapped. "I am so proud of you. Think about it, June. You saved someone's life! I'd give you a big hug, but you're all wet." June just smiled and sat down on her towel. It wasn't just a gray day. It was a *great* day!

June Gloom

It was a gray day. The sky was a sad, gray color. The sea was the same gray color, only darker. The sun was nowhere to be seen. "Fantastic," said June as she dropped her stuff on the sand. "A gray day. I cannot believe we drove all the way to the beach for this gloomy weather."

"Well, at least we don't have to worry about getting a sunburn," Ava said as she put on her cute, new sweatshirt. June looked up and down the beach.

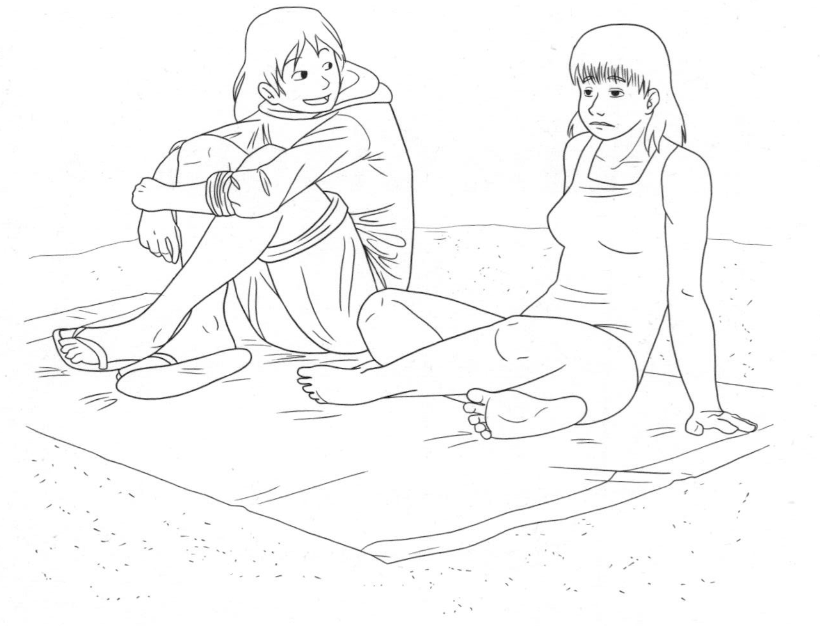

Only a few people were on the sand, and even fewer were brave enough to take a swim in the water.

"I wonder how cold it is out there," June said to Ava. "It looks really cold. That one guy is wearing a wetsuit," June

You scared us to death!" the woman shouted as she held the boy close to her. A small crowd of people began to gather on the sand. Then the man spoke to June. "Thank you so much for saving our little boy!" He had tears in his eyes as he grabbed June's hand. "Thank you so much! It all happened so fast. We didn't know what to do."

"I'm just happy I got to him in time," June said. "It was nothing, really. I'm just glad he's OK." Now several people were standing around the boy and his parents. June was so tired! All she wanted to do was to get back to her beach towel and lie down. June stepped back and slipped out of the crowd. She slowly walked back to her beach towel. Ava greeted her friend with a big smile on her face.

arm around him and started to swim again. “You just keep floating. I’ll get us out of here,” she told him. June could feel the riptide trying to pull them out to sea. She knew that she shouldn’t try to swim against it. Instead, she swam sideways, across it. June had to use all her energy to fight the waves and the current. After a few yards, she could no longer feel the pulling. That meant they were out of the riptide. It was time for her to swim to the beach, with the boy in tow. June’s arms were sore, but she just kept swimming.

At last they were in shallow water. The boy was so tired that he could barely stand up. June was just about to ask him his name when a man and a woman came running over. “Bobby, are you OK?

said as she pointed to a man on the north end of the beach. Then she looked up at the sky. “How can it be so cold and gray on the first day of summer?” June mused. She hung her head in disgust and sat down. Then she opened her picnic basket and got out a bag of chips. “Want some?” she asked Ava.

“Thanks,” said Ava as she reached into the bag. “I forgot to eat breakfast. I could use some fuel.” Ava munched on a chip while she dug a magazine out of her tote bag. “I wish we had something hot to drink. All I brought was cold soda. Silly me,” said Ava. “For some reason I thought it was going to be hot today.” They both chuckled. June stared out at the water. She loved to watch the huge waves crash. That’s when June saw a young boy who was far out in the water. She watched him for a minute or two before she realized that he was in trouble.

"Look!" June said as she pointed to the boy in the water. "I think that kid needs help. I think he's drowning!" June looked over to the lifeguard tower. But the lifeguard wasn't there! June was shocked. "Where's the lifeguard?" she yelled. "Someone has to do something!" Ava jumped up to see what June was talking about. Then she saw the boy bob up and down in the water like a cork.

"June, you have to rescue him! I'm not that strong of a swimmer. Hurry, June! Don't argue with me!" Ava pulled June up by the arm and started to drag her toward the water. Without thinking, June kicked off her shoes and started to run. June was so excited that she didn't

even notice how cold it was when she first jumped in.

June waded in the water for the first few yards. When it got deep enough, she began to swim. Every time a wave came by, she would lose sight of the boy. It made June nervous. June kept swimming. At last she was close enough to shout to him. June waved at the boy. "Are you all right? I'm coming to get you!" she yelled between two big waves. She could tell the boy could see her.

"Help!" the boy shouted. "Help! I'm stuck in a riptide. It's pulling me out to sea!" June could see that the boy was very scared. It made her swim all that much faster. At last she managed to swim over to him. "Do you know how to float?" she asked the boy. He got on his back and started floating. June got her

Name:

Long *u* & Double *o* and Open Syllables 2

Long Double *o*

In each sentence, underline the word that contains the long double ***o*** sound. Then read each sentence aloud.

1. The strong paint fumes filled the room.
2. "Boo!" shouted Pat as he jumped out from behind the bushes.
3. Joan lost one of her gold hoop earrings.
4. "I lost my first tooth!" said my nephew.
5. Please get home soon.
6. Ken and I like to shoot a few hoops at the park.

On the lines provided, write a sentence using each word given.

7. moon ______________________________

____

8. zoo ______________________________

____

9. pool ______________________________

____

10. spoon ______________________________

____

Name:

Long *u* & Double *o* and Open Syllables 2

Make a Word

Draw a line from each open syllable in the first column to the syllable that makes a word in the second column. Then write the words on the lines provided below. The first one has been done for you.

1.	a	cret
2.	se	nit
3.	u	pron
4.	be	zen
5.	re	hind
6.	fro	pen
7.	ho	mind
8.	o	bot
9.	tu	tel
10.	ro	lip

1. apron

2. ______

3. ______

4. ______

5. ______

6. ______

7. ______

8. ______

9. ______

10. ______

Name:

Long *u* & Double *o* and Open Syllables 2

Get Ready

- Sometimes we confuse *good* and *well*. The most common mistake is to use *good* when we should use *well*.

  You will not have this problem if you keep in mind the difference between an adjective and an adverb, because *good* is an *adjective*, and *well* is usually an *adverb*.

Good	**Well**
adjective	adverb
describes a noun or pronoun	describes a verb
tells *what kind of* or *what*	tells *how*

- Study these examples.

Mario is a *good* artist. He paints *well*.

What kind of artist is Mario?	*good*, adjective
How does Mario paint?	*well*, adverb

Katie throws *good* passes. She plays basketball *well*.

What kind of passes does Katie throw?	*good*, adjective
How does Katie play basketball?	*well*, adverb

Randy is a *good* dancer. He follows the music *well*.

What kind of dancer is Randy?	*good*, adjective
How does Randy follow the music?	*well*, adverb

Try It

Complete each sentence by writing the word *good* or *well* on the lines provided.

1. Philip knows how to row a boat _______________.
2. How are you today? I am _______________.
3. Did you get a _______________ grade on the math quiz?
4. We can always count on Ben to do the job _______________.
5. Is that milk still _______________ to drink?
6. Today is a _______________ day to go to the beach.
7. I don't know how to sing very _______________.
8. That was a really _______________ movie!
9. Natasha is pretty _______________ at hitting the target.
10. How _______________ do you know Dr. Martin?

Unit 19 Assessment

Part 1.

Read each word below. On the lines provided, write *Y* for *yes* if the word contains the long double *o* sound. Write *N* for *no* if the word does not contain the long double *o* sound.

1. tune ______
2. few ______
3. due ______
4. tooth ______
5. cold ______
6. nephew ______

Part 2.

Listen to each word that is read to you. Write each word in the correct column according to how the long double *o* sound is spelled in that word.

7. ***ew***	**8.** ***oo***	**9.** ***u***	**10.** ***ue***	**11.** ***u-e***

Name:

Long *u* & Double *o* and Syllable Types

Part 3.

In each row, underline the word that contains the long double *o* sound.

12.	town	tuba	tunnel
13.	gutter	goal	glue
14.	moo	mold	much
15.	could	crown	chew
16.	boat	blue	blow
17.	flute	float	flour
18.	round	room	rotten
19.	just	join	July
20.	student	stumble	stowed

Part 4.

Listen to each word that is read to you. Write each word on the lines provided.

21. ____________

22. ____________

23. ____________

24. ____________

25. ____________

Name:

Long *u* & Double *o* and Syllable Types

Part 5.

On the lines provided, write the number of syllables that each word contains.

26. over ______

27. cheese ______

28. Atlantic ______

29. behind ______

30. until ______

31. yellow ______

32. strings ______

33. volcano ______

34. faster ______

35. tulip ______

Name:

Long *u* & Double *o* and Syllable Types

Part 6.

On the lines provided, write the two syllables contained in each word and the type of syllables that they are. Use *O* for "open" syllable and *C* for "closed" syllable. An example has been done for you.

Example: hotel ho tel O, C

36. bonus ________ ________ ________

37. pilot ________ ________ ________

38. until ________ ________ ________

39. apron ________ ________ ________

40. robin ________ ________ ________

41. insect ________ ________ ________

42. belong ________ ________ ________

43. unit ________ ________ ________

44. exit ________ ________ ________

45. student ________ ________ ________

Name:

Double *o* and Open Syllables 1

Word Jumble

Read aloud each double *o* word in the box below.

hook	book	stood	good	cook	wood

Find and underline each word shown above hidden in the jumble below.
Hint: There is one double *o* word in each row of letters.

m	o	o	p	c	o	o	k
g	o	o	d	o	o	l	m
h	o	o	b	o	o	k	t
w	s	t	o	o	d	m	s
v	o	o	k	w	o	o	d
t	o	o	h	o	o	k	r

Choose two words from the top box. On the lines provided below, write a sentence using each word.

1. ______________________________

____

2. ______________________________

____

Name:

Double *o* and Open Syllables 1

Open or Closed?

Read each word pair. Decide what type of syllable the two words contain, open or closed. On the line provided, write *O* for *open* or *C* for *closed*.

Example: cup, tub ___C___

1. go, so ______

2. hit, sip ______

3. mop, hot ______

4. by, my ______

5. up, us ______

6. be, we ______

7. had, sat ______

8. spy, fly ______

Name:

Double *o* Sounds

Read each word in the word box. Write the words from the box in each column below according to the vowel sound they contain.
Hint: There are six words with the long double *o* sound, and there are six words with the short double *o* sound.

cook	tooth	tool	foot	stood	took
good	root	wood	broom	gloom	hoop

Long Double *o*	Short Double *o*
______________	______________
______________	______________
______________	______________
______________	______________
______________	______________
______________	______________

Practice Open Syllables

Read the words in the box aloud. Underline each word that contains an open syllable.

gopher	push	bacon	insect
robin	student	robot	be
exit	sunny	itself	even
she	enter	hotel	basin

Read the words in the box aloud. Underline the letter that makes the long vowel sound in the open syllable in each word.

study	we	remind	pretty
begin	relax	silent	tulip
fly	frozen	unit	paper
over	acorn	secret	hello

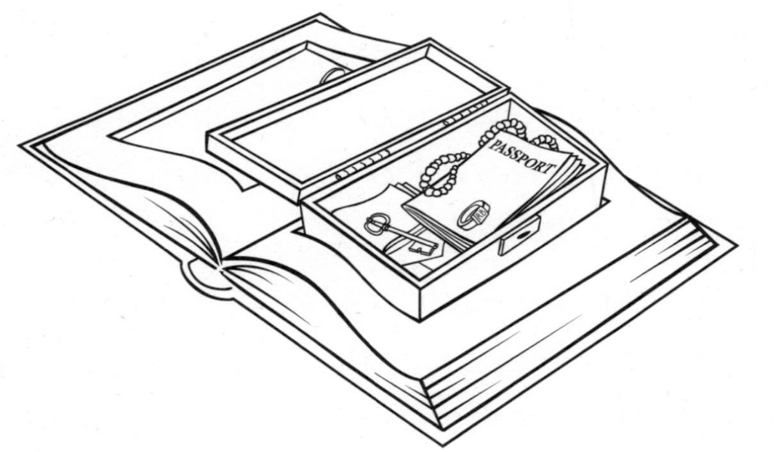

who killed Mr. Brook." Dad looked down at the game fondly. Then he glanced at Jay. "I know! How about you and I try to solve it together? You seem to be interested."

"That's a great idea, Dad!" said Jay. "You know I love a mystery!"

The Book of Secrets

It was a rainy afternoon, and Jay was bored. He had finished all of his homework. Nothing good was on TV. He didn't feel like playing a computer game. His brother was at work, and all his friends were busy. What could he do to amuse himself? Jay let out a sigh. He got up off his bed and wandered down the hall to the family room. He stood at the doorway for a moment and stared.

Then he went over to the old, wooden bookcase to look for something to read. The bookcase was as big as the entire wall.

Jay walked back and forth in front of the bookcase. So many books! He ran his finger along the spines of the books

stared at each other for a moment. Then Jay let out a big laugh.

"OK, you got me!" Jay said. "I thought I found a hidden treasure or something!" Now Dad was laughing, too. Then Dad's eyes lit up.

"I know! We put the rest of the game in that cabinet over there." Dad ran over to the cabinet and pulled out a tattered, old box. "See, here it is!" he shouted with joy. Jay looked up and saw the name of the game on the side of the box: *The Book of Secrets—A Murder Mystery*. Dad brought the box over to the table and set it down. Inside were playing cards, a game board, a pair of dice, an instruction book, and little tokens for each player. "Looks like everything is still here," Dad said, smiling. "Your mother and I spent hours trying to figure how

"Sure. It's part of a board game we bought years ago," Dad said. "You were just a kid when your mother and I got it." Dad looked around the room. "I wonder where the rest of it is?" he mumbled as he scratched his head. "It's lots of fun. Those things inside of the book are clues to solve a murder mystery." Dad looked back over at Jay. "Now that I think about it, I'm not sure we ever figured out who did it."

"You mean all of this stuff is fake?" Jay asked in shock. He looked down at all of the items on the table. "This is part of a game?"

"Yeah, it was pretty popular a few years back," Dad replied. "Why? What did you think it was?" he asked. "Did you think this was for real?" Dad and Jay

as he scanned the titles. History books. Cook books. Story books. Art books. Poetry books. Mystery books. Law books. Picture books. Jay was surprised at how many he had already read. *Maybe there's something up here*, Jay said to himself as he looked at the very top shelf. All he saw were more books that he had already read. Jay was about to give up when he happened to see a book in the corner that was new to him. It looked very old. In fact, it was so old the title was worn off the spine of the book. All that was left were a few flecks of gold paint where the letters used to be. Jay stood on the tips of his toes and reached for it. The book seemed much too light for its size, and it made a noise when he pulled it out from the shelf.

What is this? Jay didn't watch what he was doing and lost his grip. The book fell to the floor with a bang, just missing his foot. The book flipped open. Then Jay's mouth fell open with surprise. It wasn't a book at all. It was a book *safe*, a book with a secret compartment. Jay had heard about these things, but he never saw one before. Jay bent down to pick it up. Then he shook it. Jay could hear something rattle inside.

Jay took the book over to the card table and sat down. He saw a small latch on the lid to the secret compartment. He held his breath and pushed down on the latch. The lid popped open. Jay felt a thrill rush through him. Jay peeked inside. He saw many things. He pulled them out, one by one, and laid them on the table. A man's gold ring with

the letters "R. B." carved in it. An old passport. A pearl necklace. A matchbook with "White Tulip" on the label. An odd tool with a little hook on the end of it. At the bottom of the compartment was an old letter. Jay took out the letter and unfolded it with care. Then he began to read aloud. *My name is Mr. Ronald Brook. If you have found this letter, it means I am dead.* Jay gasped. His heart began to pound. He read on. *My story begins in London, England. I own an import-export business. But I am really a spy.* Jay was about to read the next line when someone walked into the room. Jay almost jumped out of his seat.

"Oh, I see you found *The Book of Secrets,*" Dad said. "I forgot all about that."

"What? You know about this book and this letter?" Jay asked. He was confused.

Unit 20 Assessment

Part 1.

Read each word below. On the lines provided, write *Y* for *yes* if the word contains the sound /o͝o/. Write *N* for *no* if the word does not contain the sound /o͝o/.

1. shook ______
2. bloom ______
3. wood ______
4. fool ______
5. loop ______
6. good ______
7. zoo ______
8. woof ______
9. toot ______
10. look ______

Assessment

Name:

Double *o* and Syllable Types

Part 2.

In each row, underline the word that contains the sound /$\overline{oo}$/.

11. foot food

12. boot book

13. cool cook

14. hood hoop

15. tool took

Part 3.

Listen to each word that is read to you. Write each word on the lines provided.

16. ____________

17. ____________

18. ____________

19. ____________

20. ____________

21. ____________

22. ____________

23. ____________

24. ____________

25. ____________

Name:

Double *o* and Syllable Types

Part 4.

On the lines provided, write the number of syllables that each word contains.

26. pretty ______

27. scream ______

28. animals ______

29. glance ______

30. sisters ______

31. twice ______

32. alphabet ______

33. boxes ______

Part 5.

Underline the vowel-consonant-*e* syllable that makes the word complete. Then, write the completed word on the line provided. An example has been done for you.

Example:	in	sive	<u>side</u>	inside
34.	mis	take	teke	______________
35.	cos	tome	tume	______________
36.	sun	shine	shene	______________
37.	cup	cake	cace	______________

Name:

Double *o* and Syllable Types

Part 6.

On the lines provided, write the two syllables contained in each word and the type of syllables that they are. Write *O* for "open" syllable, *C* for "closed" syllable, and *V-C-E* for "vowel-consonant-*e*" syllable. An example has been done for you.

Example: inside ____in____ ____side____ ____C, V-C-E____

38. paper ________ ________ ________

39. happy ________ ________ ________

40. basement ________ ________ ________

41. gopher ________ ________ ________

42. rosebud ________ ________ ________

43. fireplace ________ ________ ________

44. tulip ________ ________ ________

45. sunrise ________ ________ ________

46. secret ________ ________ ________

47. snakeskin ________ ________ ________

48. apron ________ ________ ________

49. baby ________ ________ ________

Get Ready

- **Adverbs** are words that can be used to *describe*, or *modify*, verbs. Some adverbs tell *how* the action of a verb takes place. This kind of adverb often ends in *–ly*, and it can come before or after the verb in a sentence. For example:

  Janette spoke *loudly* on the phone.
  (*How* did Janette speak? Loudly.)

  My brother *quietly* cried in his room.
  (*How* did my brother cry? Quietly.)

  Bravely, the man walked into the lion's cage.
  (*How* did the man walk? Bravely.)

  Brenda pressed the doorbell *firmly*.
  (*How* did Brenda press the doorbell? Firmly.)

- Study this list of adverbs that that end in *–ly* and can be used to modify a verb.

quickly	loudly	softly	slowly
nicely	sadly	carefully	easily
silently	firmly	cheerfully	warmly
rudely	weakly	painfully	bravely
badly	quietly	calmly	safely

Name:

Try It

In each sentence, underline the verb and circle the adverb that modifies it.

1. The big tiger ran quickly through the jungle.
2. The angry man stared calmly at the cop.
3. Jamie yelled loudly during the whole game.
4. Bart carefully shut the glass door.
5. The butterfly landed softly on the flower petal.
6. Sadly, Mom told us our trip was canceled.
7. Kurt smiled at his dance partner weakly.
8. My sister whispered quietly in my ear.
9. Carefully, the dentist drilled the tooth.
10. "I won the race!" Jason shouted to his parents proudly.

Name:

Schwa and V-C-E Syllables 1

Schwa Sound

Choose the word from the box that best matches each definition. Write the word on the line next to the definition. In each word, underline the vowel that makes the schwa sound.

alone	lemon	pizza	ribbon	wagon	awake	puma

1. not asleep ____________
2. a bitter, yellow fruit ____________
3. a large, wild, fast cat ____________
4. fabric used to tie into a bow ____________
5. separate or away from others ____________
6. a four-wheeled cart used for pulling heavy loads ____________
7. an Italian food that is usually round, with toppings of tomatoes, cheese, and spices ____________

Name:

Schwa and V-C-E Syllables 1

Syllable Match-Ups

Match a syllable from the "Syllable 1" box to a syllable in the "Syllable 2" box to make a real word. Write each word on the lines provided in the "Words" box and then read the words aloud. An example has been done for you.

Syllable 1	Syllable 2	Words
ath	pede	**Example:** athlete
stam	fuse	______
ex	lete	______
con	plode	______

Syllable 1	Syllable 2	Words
com	vide	______
pro	tile	______
rep	side	______
in	bine	______

Syllable 1	Syllable 2	Words
cos	flate	______
be	rise	______
in	have	______
sun	tume	______

big sigh as she turned on the car heater. She found a towel in the glove box and handed it to her mother. Mom began to dab the cut on the top of her head. "What a complete nightmare!" she said. She looked over at Sue with a weak smile. "Next time, let's turn on that radio of yours *before* we go sailing!"

The End of Mona

Sue was thrilled. Mom had just agreed to take her out on the lake. Sue loved to sail with her mother. They would glide out on the water where they could be all alone. Sometimes they would just sit and talk. Other times they would fish for hours without saying a word. The last time they sailed, Sue sat and read an entire book aloud to her mother. No matter what they did, Sue always had a good time on the lake.

Mom started to load the car. Sue said she had to run down to the basement to get her new shortwave radio. "OK, if you think we need it. But make it quick!" Mom said. "I'm just about done here." Sue opened the basement door and rushed down the stairs. *Where is it?*

instant. Sue tossed her radio inside, then she jumped in, too. After she helped her mother step in, Sue put the oars in their holders. Sue was no athlete, but she was determined to row the life raft all the way to shore by herself. "Goodbye, *Mona*!" Mom said sadly as she watched the sailboat sink into the water. But Sue was too busy worrying about getting ashore to look back.

Sue's arms started to burn about halfway across the lake. She told herself it would be over soon and to just keep rowing. By now, rain was coming down hard and the lake was filled with waves. Somehow they made it back to the dock. Sue and her mother could not wait to get out of the raft and back on land. They dragged the raft out of the water and ran to the car. Sue let out a over the stern. Sue looked down at her feet. "Mom, look!" she yelled as she jumped up. "We're taking on water!" All of a sudden, a big gust of wind made the main sail swing around. The boom hit Mom right in the head. "Mom!" shouted Sue as her mother fell onto the deck. "Mom, are you OK?" Sue yelled as she bent over to help. Now Sue was really scared.

"I'm OK, honey. It didn't hurt that bad," Mom said as she held her hand to her head. "Don't worry about me. We need to get off this boat *now*!" Sue scrambled over to the portside bench. She pulled out the old life raft that was stored below it. Sue held tight to the cord and tossed the compressed raft into the water. She gave the cord a big yank. *Whoosh!* The raft inflated with air in an

she wondered to herself. Sue wanted to bring along her new radio because it was waterproof. It would also stay afloat if it fell overboard. At last she saw it tucked under Dad's workbench. Sue grabbed the radio and rushed back upstairs. She ran into her bedroom and found a ribbon to tie her long hair back into a ponytail. Sue was about to head outside when she saw that the basement door was ajar. Sue kicked the door shut with her foot. *Now* she was ready to leave!

Sue and her mother were at the lake in less than an hour. They took the picnic basket, radio, and other items out of the car. Then they walked down to the dock to look for the *Mona*. Dad had named their boat after his mother. Sue thought that was sweet. It was a small boat, with only two sails. The *Mona* was just the perfect size for two adults. They came aboard and put down all their stuff. Then they put on their life jackets. Mom raised the sails. Next, Sue untied the boat from the dock. Everything was set. Sue leaned over the side of the boat and put her hand on the dock. One. Two. Three. *Push!* The boat began to float away. At last they were sailing!

It was a sunny, but windy, day on the lake. Sue sat on the starboard bench. Mom sat aft and took care of the sails and the rudder. They drifted so far out that Sue could barely see the shore of the lake when she looked up from her book. It made her feel like they were all alone in the world. "Gee, it's getting really windy," Sue said aloud as she looked out over the lake. "And the water

is so choppy." Mom nodded. There was a frown on her face. Mom pointed to the west with her free hand. Sue turned around to look. What Sue saw scared her. There was a row of thick, black clouds off in the distance, and they were getting bigger by the minute. Sue could swear she saw a flash of lightning, too!

"Those clouds look like trouble," Mom said. "Turn on your radio, Sue. Try to find the weather report." Sue put her book aside. She reached for the radio and fiddled with the dial. After a minute or two, Sue shouted to her mother with alarm.

"Oh, no! It's a big storm! They're warning people not to take their boats out on the lake! We better head back, Mom!" Just then, a big wave washed over the deck. Then another wave broke

Name:

Schwa and V-C-E Syllables 2

Words with the Schwa Sound

Choose a word from the box that means the same or almost the same as the word or words below. Write the words on the lines provided. Then underline the letter that makes the schwa sound in each word you wrote.

afraid	data	pasta	scuba	wagon	above	drama

1. cart ______________
2. over ______________
3. a play ______________
4. scared ______________
5. spaghetti ______________
6. information ______________
7. underwater diving equipment ______________

Sentences

Choose three words from the box above. On the lines provided, write a sentence using each word and then read the sentences aloud.

8. ____

9. ____

10. ____

Name:

Schwa and V-C-E Syllables 2

Vowel-Consonant-*e* Syllables

Match one vowel-consonant-*e* syllable from the box to each of the syllables below to form a two-syllable word. Write each syllable on the lines provided. Then read each word aloud.

base	cake	lete	note	tile
race	shake	take	rise	side

1. ath__________
2. __________ball
3. cup__________
4. hand__________
5. in__________
6. mis__________
7. __________book
8. __________track
9. sun__________
10. rep__________

camera. I want to take a picture first." Mom ran to get her camera. She was back in no time. "Scooter, it's your cake. How about you blow out the candles and make a wish?" Scooter jumped up. Mom snapped a picture as she blew out the candles. And no one had to ask what Scooter wished for!

The Secret Project

Bruce was in the kitchen all by himself. He was working on a secret project. No one was allowed to come in until he was done. Bruce even pinned a sign on the kitchen door. It read:

TOP SECRET. DO NOT ENTER!

It all started last May. Scooter, Bruce's little sister, saw a TV show about a volcano in Hawaii. Ever since then she wanted to go see the volcano. It's all she talked about for days and days.

Mom and Dad finally said that the family could go to Hawaii this year for summer vacation. Scooter was so excited! But Mom's car broke down the very next week. Dad said they had to use the money for the trip to buy

"Thanks!" Bruce said. He quickly added the orange candy spikes to the top of the cake. Done! Dad swung open the door. Then Bruce picked up his masterpiece and walked into the dining room. Everyone gasped. Scooter smiled for the first time in days.

"Oh! What is that, Bruce?" shouted his little sister. The orange spikes sparkled in the candlelight.

"Volcano Cake!" Bruce shouted. He beamed with pride. "I made it just for you, Scooter. I got the idea while I was watching a cooking show last night. If we can't go visit the volcano, then the volcano can come visit us!" Everyone stared in awe at the volcano cake.

"It's so wonderful! I don't want to cut into it," Mom said. "Let me get my

room table. Bruce turned off the lights and went back into the kitchen to get his secret project. "Dad, could you come in here for a second?" Bruce yelled. Dad got up and walked into the kitchen.

"What's up? Dad asked. "I thought this was a big secret and no one gets to see what you're doing in here."

"I need you to light some candles. Mom still doesn't like me using matches," Bruce said. Dad looked at the secret project. He smiled, but he didn't say anything. Dad took the book of matches and lit the candles one by one. Bruce took the time to wipe some batter off his face.

"OK, you're all set," Dad said when he was finished. "Looks like you'll have your hands full. I'll hold the door open for you."

a new car instead. Mom and Dad said the family would have to wait until next year to go see the volcano. But Scooter didn't care. She wanted to see a volcano now! Scooter had moped around the house ever since then. And that was two weeks ago!

Last night, Bruce got an idea. He figured out a way to cheer up his little sister. That's what his secret project was all about. Bruce looked around the kitchen. First he got together all the things he needed to make a cake. Then he got out three cake pans. Two were the usual round cake pans. The third one was a special pan that makes a tall cake. It's called an angel food cake pan. Bruce used two boxes of cake mix for the batter. He poured the batter into the

© 2010 K12 Inc. All rights reserved.

pans. Then he put the pans in the oven. Bruce made a big batch of chocolate frosting while the cakes baked. When the cakes were done, Bruce put them near an open window so they would cool fast. Then he sat down and ate a tuna sandwich. Baking is hard work!

The cakes were cold by the time Bruce finished eating. Now the fun began. Bruce popped each cake out of its pan. He put the two round cakes on top of each other on a cake stand. Then he put the tall cake on top of the round cakes. It made one big cake. Bruce cut the sides of the big cake so they sloped. He stepped back and looked at his work. Bruce made a few more cuts. He looked at it again. Perfect! Now he started to frost the sides and top of the big cake. When that was done, he opened a bag

of rock candy that he had bought at the store. He put the fake rocks all around the base of the cake. Next he got out a bag of hard candy. Bruce picked out all the orange pieces and put them in a sauce pan. Then he put the pan on the stove so they started to melt. When they were all gooey, he poured the melted candy onto a cookie sheet. He poured the candy into the shape of long, jagged spikes. While the spikes cooled, Bruce pushed candles into the top of the cake. The last thing Bruce did was to sweep up the flour off the floor with a broom. Then he put all the dirty bowls and spoons in the dishwasher. That way Mom couldn't complain that he left a mess in her kitchen. Bruce was just about done. He found everyone and told them to sit down at the dining

Name: ______

Schwa and V-C-E Syllables 3

Find the Schwa Sound

Choose the word from the box that matches each description. Write the word on the line after the description.
Hint: Some descriptions will match two words. In those cases, write both words.

afraid	banana	ago	collide
alone	item	awake	sofa

1. has a long *o* sound in the first syllable and ends with a schwa sound ______
2. begins with a schwa sound and has a long *a* sound in the second syllable ______
3. has a schwa sound in two syllables ______
4. has a long *i* sound in the first syllable and has a schwa sound in the second syllable ______
5. begins with a schwa sound and has a long *o* sound in the second syllable ______
6. has a schwa sound in the first syllable and has a long *i* sound in the second syllable ______

Name: ____________________

Vowel-Consonant-*e* Syllables

Underline each syllable in the box that is a vowel-consonant-*e* syllable.

ap	use	cake	fle	side
home	sud	space	base	vict

On the first line in each group, write the vowel-consonant-*e* syllable from the box above that correctly completes the group of words. Then complete each word in the group with the correct syllable. The first one has been done for you.

1. base
base ball
base ment

2. ____________
in____________
out____________
____________walk

3. ____________
pan____________
cup____________

4. ____________
____________craft
____________ship
____________suit

5. ____________
____________made
____________sick
____________work

6. ____________
____________ful
____________less

"Are you kidding?" Jack replied. "I can't wait to try it again!" he shouted with joy. "You couldn't keep me away from it!"

"Just like when we were kids!" said Tom as he shook his head and smiled. "Just like when we were kids!"

The Big Dipper

Tom awoke to the sound of a loud bell. He opened his eyes and turned off the alarm clock. It was just before sunrise. *Time to get up!* he thought to himself with glee. Tom was an adult, but he felt like a kid again. He was going to the state fair today! Tom jumped out of bed. "I can't wait to get on thos rides!" he said aloud. Tom put on a T-shirt and shorts. Then he ran out the bedroom door. He gulped down a glass of milk and ate a cupcake. He put the glass in the sink and checked his watch. *Time to go!*

Tom got in his car and drove down the street to Jack's house. Tom and Jack had been friends since they were five years old. Tom was about to honk the horn when he saw Jack standing at the curb. Jack got into the car and pulled out a map. "Let's go!" he said. "We need to get on the freeway so we can get there ahead of the crowds."

"How long did you stand outside?" asked Tom. "Was I late?"

"Only for a little while," said Jack. "I didn't even think about it. You are *always* on time," he said with a smile. "'On-Time Tom'—that could be your nickname," Jack joked. He looked at the

cage without a scratch. Jack was fine, too, but he looked a bit confused.

"You want to go on it again?" laughed Tom. "Or do you want to try another one? Maybe you want to get something to eat first?"

"A corn dog sounds good to me," said Tom. "All that screaming made me super hungry!" The friends sniffed the air to find the closest corn dog stand. They got their food and sat down at a table. Jack popped open a bottle of water and took a sip. "I have to tell you, that ride scared me bad!" he said to Tom. "I wasn't aware I had such a fear of heights until now!"

"I hope you're not saying you don't want to go back on it again," Tom said. He sounded a little upset.

Jack by the arm and pulled him inside the cage. They buckled their seat belts and held on to the safety bars. The cage jerked forward and the ride began to move. Jack's eyes grew wide with fear. They went up, up, up into the air. Then the cage began to flip around so they were upside down, then right-side up again. When their cage was high above the skyline, they started to fall fast. And all the while the cage kept flipping over and over. Tom was so filled with joy that he began to giggle. "This is the most fun I have had in years!" he shouted. But Jack couldn't hear a word Tom said because he was screaming so loud. At last the cage stopped moving and Tom and Jack stumbled out the door. Aside from hitting his head, Tom came out of the

map and told Tom which way to go. "This is going to be fun. Just like when we were kids!"

"You got that right! What's the first thing you want to do when we get there?" Tom asked Jack. "There are so many things to see!"

"Do you want to start with the *Big Dipper*?" Jack asked Tom. "I hear it is the best ride at the fair."

"I heard about that one!" Tom shouted. "It sounds really fun! I hear that they put you in some sort of cage. Then they turn on the ride, and you flip up, down, and around, over and over again. Are you sure you can handle that?" Tom joked.

"You bet I can!" said Jack. "It sounds like the perfect ride to me!"

"I agree! Perfect!" said Jack. The friends talked about the different rides all the way to the fair. They were surprised when it was time to pull off the freeway. The time went by so fast!

"I'm glad we planned to get here first thing in the morning. "Look! Front-row parking!" Jack said as he pointed to a prime space. They parked the car and walked over to the main gate. After they paid for their tickets, Tom and Jack looked around for the *Big Dipper*. The ride wasn't hard to find at all. When they saw it among the other rides, it looked like a complete monster. It was early, so not many people were in front of them in line. "Wow, this is a little scary!" said Jack as he looked up to the top of the ride. He could hear people screaming and laughing inside the cages as they sped by. "I'm not sure this is such a good idea, after all. I think I'm a bit afraid to go on it!"

"Too late, now, buddy. It's our turn to get in a cage!" said Tom. He grabbed

Name:

Unit 21 Assessment

Part 1.

Underline each word in the box that contains the schwa sound.

1.

aware	collide	follow	gallop	hilltop
keyhole	leaky	pencil	ribbon	sister

Part 2.

Listen to each word that is read to you. Write each word on the lines provided.

2. ______________

3. ______________

4. ______________

5. ______________

6. ______________

Name:

Schwa and Syllable Types

Part 3. In each row, underline the word that contains the schwa sound.

7.	almost	adult	after
8.	ballad	backpack	bedroom
9.	camper	counting	connect
10.	dragon	darkness	deeper
11.	afraid	artist	asked
12.	mother	mailbox	manmade
13.	older	onto	occur
14.	safety	sofa	surfing
15.	warmer	weekend	wagon
16.	aimed	ago	arched

Name:

Schwa and Syllable Types

Part 4.

On the lines provided, write the number of syllables that each word contains.

17. alarm ______

18. butterfly ______

19. dawn ______

20. folded ______

21. around ______

22. gasp ______

23. hardest ______

24. urgently ______

25. awake ______

26. wilderness ______

Part 5.

Underline the vowel-consonant-*e* syllable in each word.

27. basement

28. female

29. homemade

30. mistake

31. outline

32. rosebush

33. sidewalk

34. beehive

35. stovetop

36. birdcage

Name:

Schwa and Syllable Types

Part 6.

In each row, underline the word that contains *at least one* vowel-consonant-*e* syllable.

37.	puppet	pumpkin	perfume
38.	campfire	countdown	carload
39.	downhill	dugout	driveway
40.	fireplace	fitness	foolproof
41.	hilltop	hopeful	halfway
42.	nickname	napkin	nearby
43.	paintbrush	pinecone	payment
44.	snapshot	subway	sunshine
45.	tadpole	tiptoe	toothbrush
46.	pancake	penny	piglet

Name:

Get Ready

- An **abbreviation** is a short way to write a word. Abbreviations save time and space in writing.

  Abbreviations for **addresses** begin with a capital letter and end with a period. For example:

Street (St.)	Drive (Dr.)	Boulevard (Blvd.)
Road (Rd.)	Place (Pl.)	Avenue (Ave.)
Parkway (Pkwy.)	Lane (Ln.)	North (N.)
South (S.)	East (E.)	West (W.)

- Abbreviations for **state names** consist of two capital letters without a period. For example:

California (CA)	Texas (TX)	Virginia (VA)

- Abbreviations for **units of measure** are unusual because, in most cases, they do not use capital letters or end with periods. However, you do use a period to abbreviate *inch* (in.) For example:

foot (ft)	yard (yd)	mile (mi)
pint (pt)	quart (qt)	gallon (gal)
second (sec)	minute (min)	pound (lb)

- Abbreviations for **days of the week** begin with a capital letter and end with a period.

Sunday (Sun.)	Wednesday (Wed.)	Saturday (Sat.)
Monday (Mon.)	Thursday (Thurs.)	Sunday (Sun.)
Tuesday (Tues.)	Friday (Fri.)	

Name:

- Abbreviations for **months of the year** begin with a capital letter and end with a period. *May*, *June*, and *July* do not have abbreviations because they are already short enough.

January (Jan.)	September (Sept.)
February (Feb.)	October (Oct.)
March (Mar.)	November (Nov.)
April (Apr.)	December (Dec.)
August (Aug.)	

- An abbreviation for a person's **title** comes before his or her name. When a title is abbreviated, it is capitalized and usually ends with a period.

Title	Use Before the Name of	Example
Ms.	single or married women	Ms. Linda Kaplar
Mrs.	married women	Mrs. Gail Tanner
Mr.	single or married men	Mr. Robert Jansen
Dr.	doctors or dentists	Dr. Maria Gonzalez

Try It

1. Rewrite the following address using abbreviations:

   17 North Fields Lane ______________________

2. Underline the correct abbreviation for *quart*.

   qu qt qrt.

3. Underline the correct abbreviation for *Tuesday*.

   Tue Tues Tues.

4. Underline the correct abbreviation for *January*.

   Jan Jan. Jany.

MARK[12] Reading I Review

Part 1.

Listen to each word that is read to you. On the lines provided, write *a*, *e*, *i*, *o*, or *u* for the short vowel sound heard in each word.

1. ______
2. ______
3. ______
4. ______
5. ______
6. ______
7. ______
8. ______
9. ______
10. ______

Part 2.

Listen to each word that is read to you. On the lines provided, write the vowels that are missing from each word.

11. ______t
12. ch______ck
13. g______ft
14. ______n
15. ______n
16. p______tch
17. s______cks
18. tr______ck
19. ______s
20. w______ll

Name:

MARK[12] Reading I Review

Part 3.

Read the words below. In each word, underline the letter or letters that make the long vowel sound.

21. brave

22. cold

23. few

24. huge

25. me

26. shield

27. tie

28. mile

29. toe

30. tray

Part 4.

Listen to each word that is read to you. Write each word on the lines provided.

31. ____________

32. ____________

33. ____________

34. ____________

35. ____________

36. ____________

37. ____________

38. ____________

39. ____________

40. ____________

Part 5.

Listen to each word that is read to you. In each row, underline the beginning blend that is contained in each word.

41. sm sn scr spl spr str

42. sm sn scr spl spr str

43. sm sn scr spl spr str

44. sm sn scr spl spr str

45. sm sn scr spl spr str

Part 6.

Listen to each word that is read to you. Write each word on the lines provided.

46. ______________

47. ______________

48. ______________

49. ______________

50. ______________

Name:

Part 7.

Read each word. Decide what type of syllable the *first* syllable is in each word. On the line provided, write *C* for *closed*, *O* for *open*, or *V-C-E* for *vowel-consonant*-e.

51. hammer ____________

52. moment ____________

53. frozen ____________

54. jacket ____________

55. open ____________

56. racetrack ____________

57. homemade ____________

58. picnic ____________

59. baseball ____________

60. winter ____________

Part 8.

In each row, underline the word that is read to you.

61.	in	it	is
62.	of	on	or
63.	where	who	with
64.	said	so	she
65.	we	want	what

Part 9.

Read each word aloud.

66. does

67. were

68. gone

69. above

70. more

Color Tiles

Capital Letters

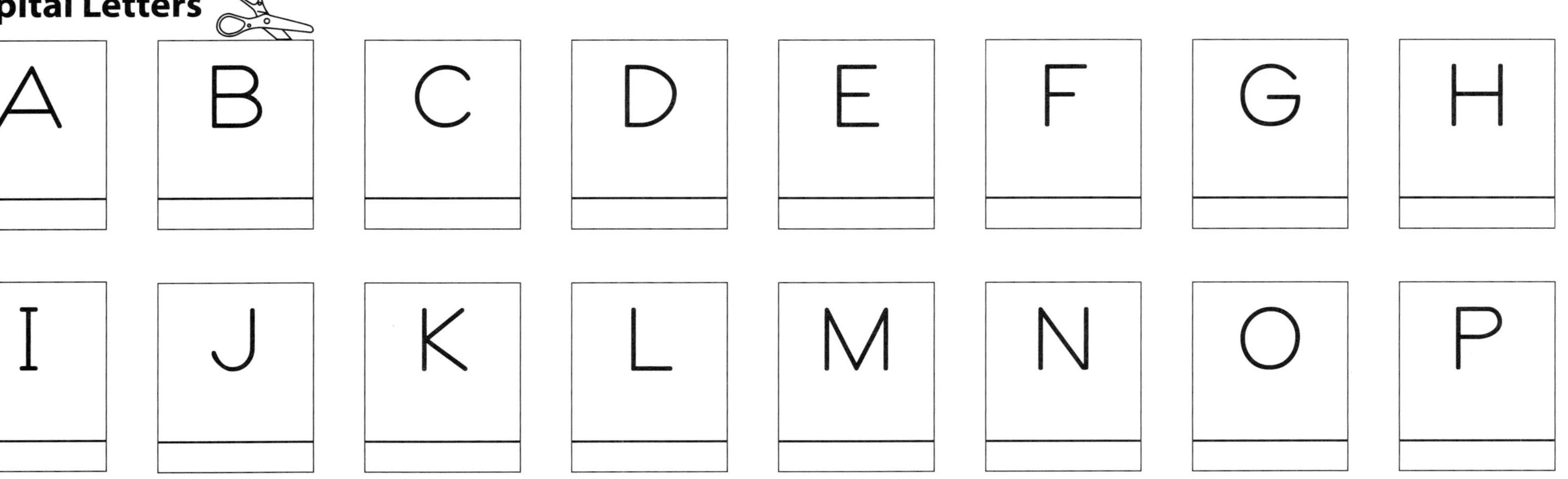

Q R S T U V W X

Y Z

Lowercase Letters

a a a a a b b b

c c c d d d d e

e	e	e	e	f	f	f	f
g	g	g	h	h	h	i	i
i	i	i	j	j	j	k	k
k	l	l	l	l	m	m	m
n	n	n	o	o	o	o	o

p p p qu qu qu r

r r s s s s t t

t u u u u u v v

v w w w x x x y

y y y z z z

Punctuation Marks

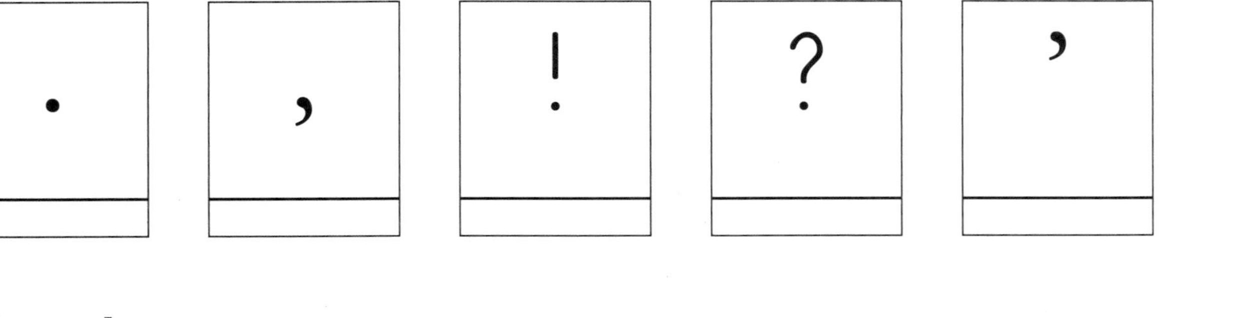

. , ! ? ’

Digraphs

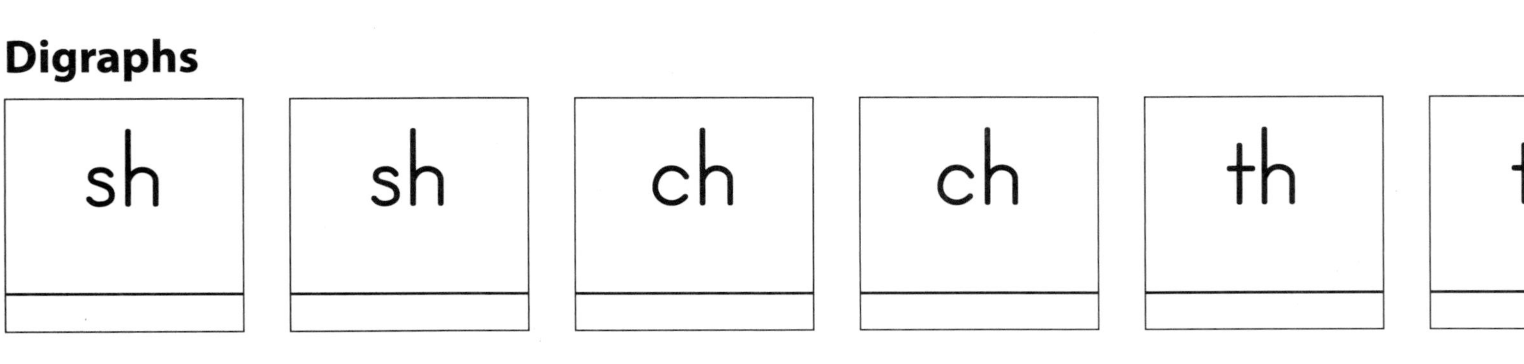

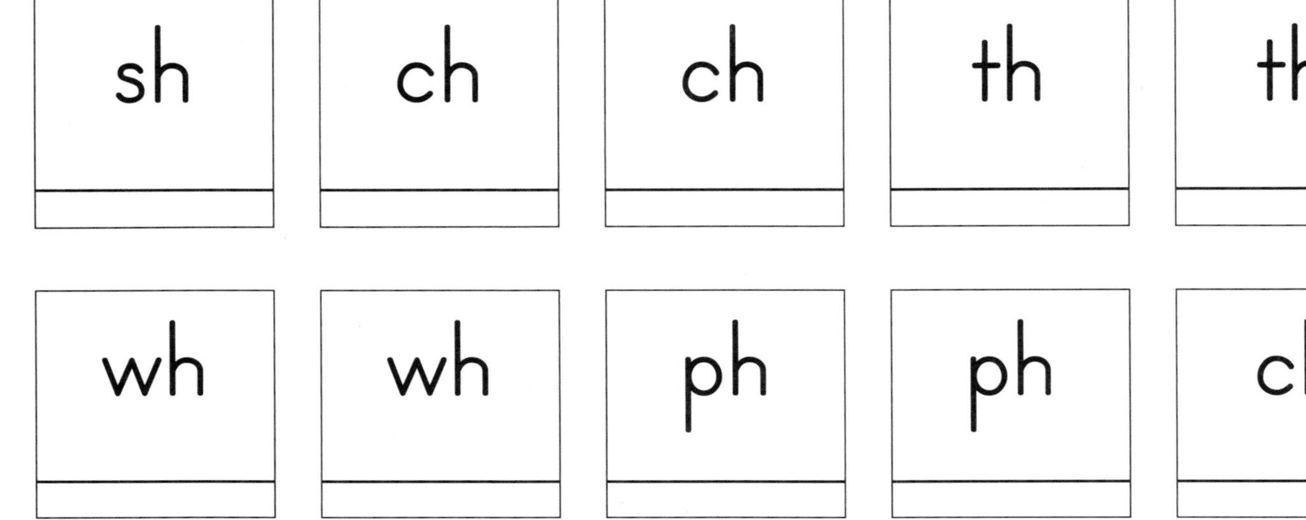

sh sh ch ch th th th

th wh wh ph ph ck ck

Trigraphs

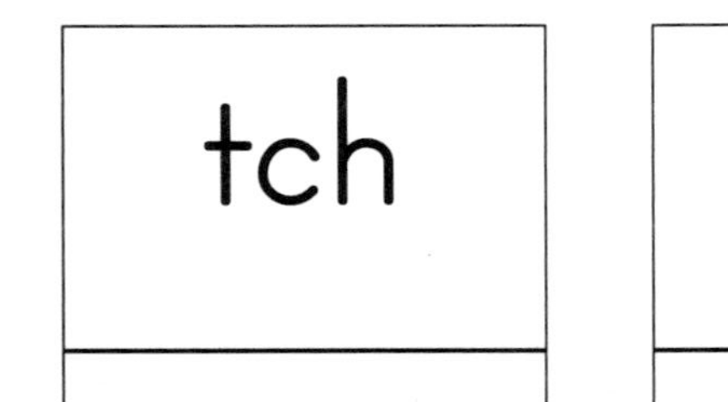

tch tch

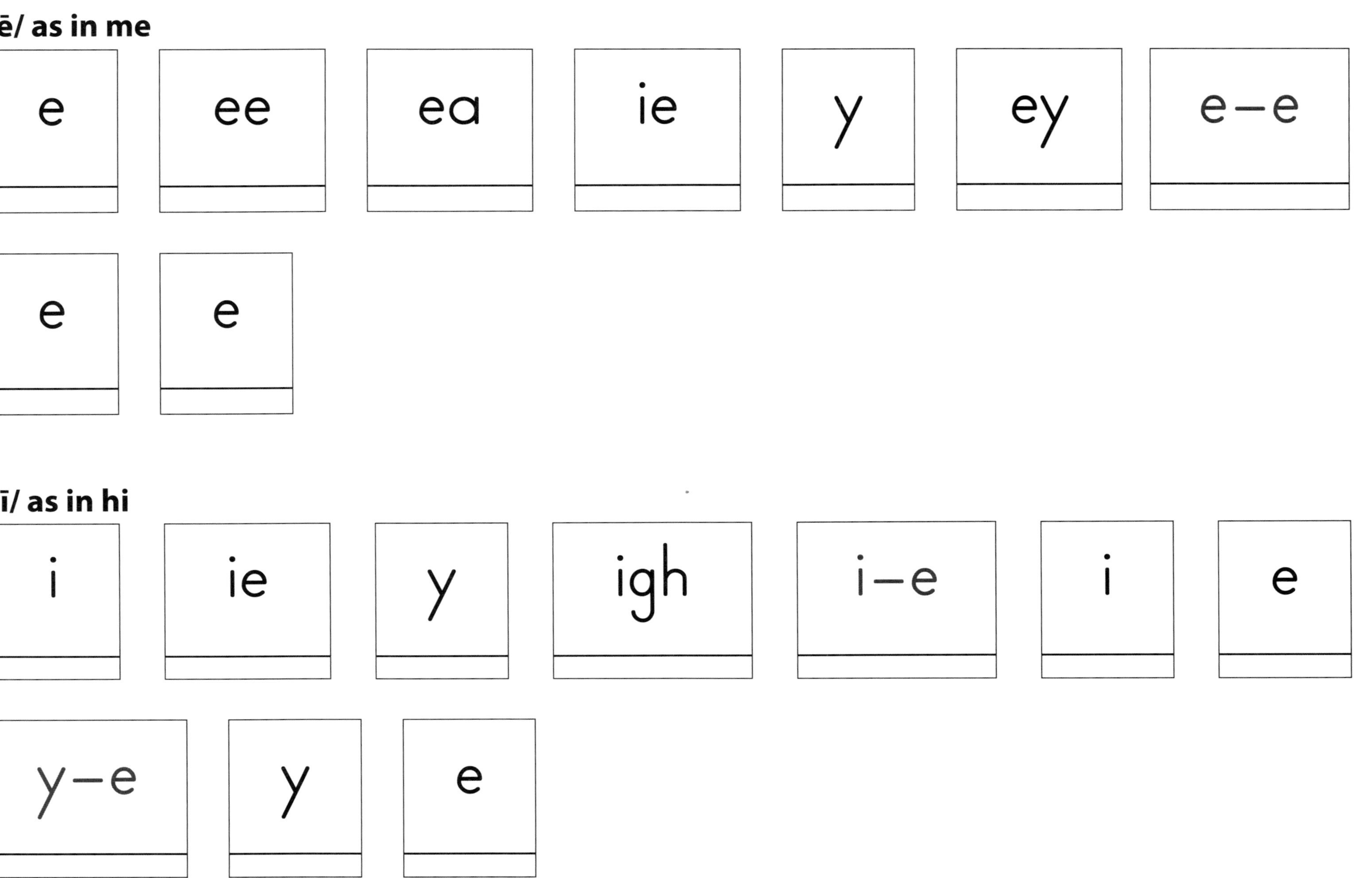
/ē/ as in me
e
ee
ea
ie
y
ey
e–e
e
e
/ī/ as in hi
i
ie
y
igh
i–e
i
e
y–e
y
e

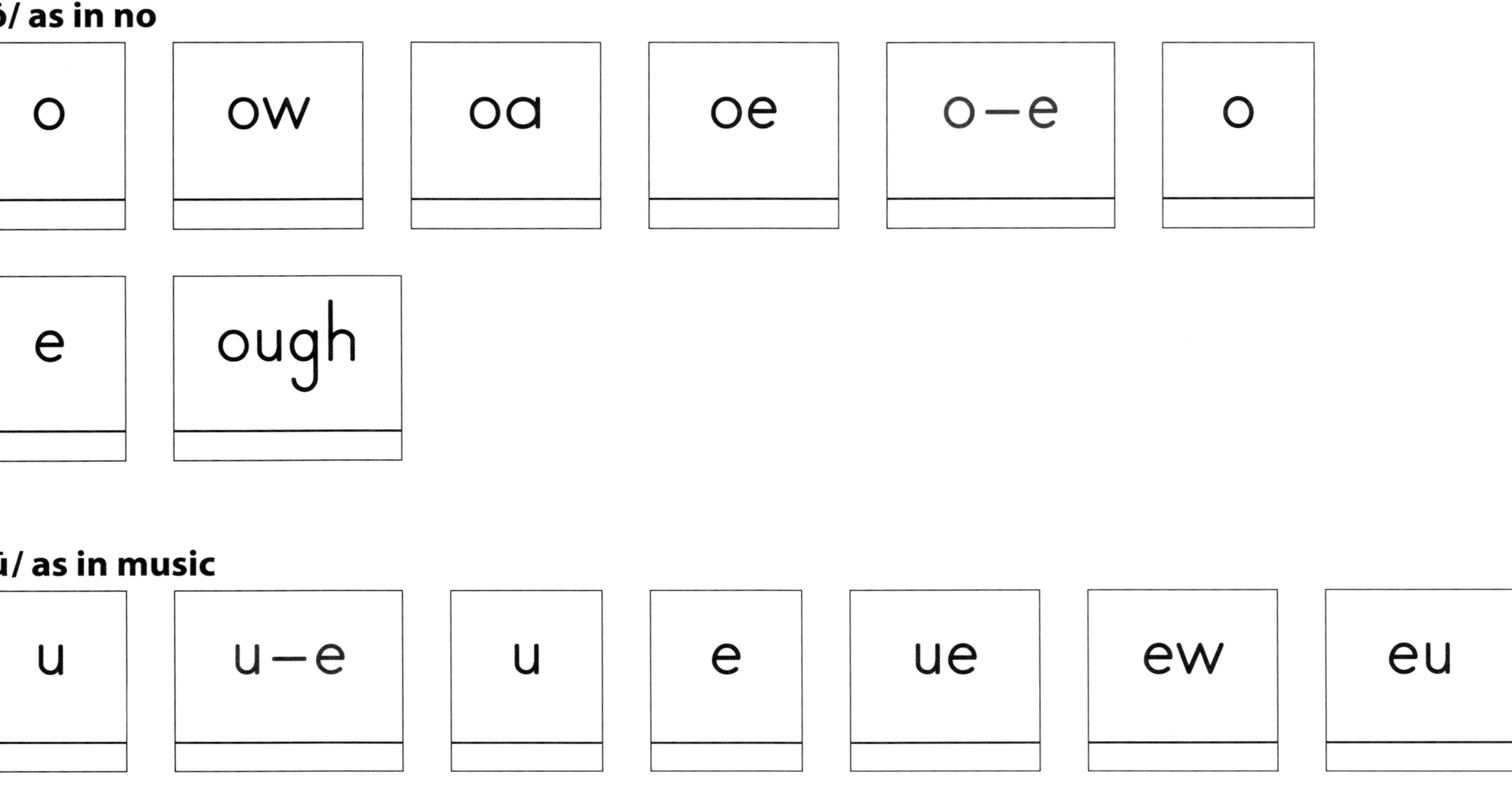
/ō/ as in no
o
ow
oa
oe
o–e
o
e
ough
/ū/ as in music
u
u–e
u
e
ue
ew
eu

/o͞o/ as in boot

oo | u | ue | ew | u–e | u

e | ough

/o͝o/ as in book

oo | u | ou

schwa

/ə/

/ar/ as in car

ar

/or/ as in for

ar | or | oar | ore

/er/ as in her

ar	er	ir	or	ur	ear

suffix –ed endings (as in hunted, sailed, and jumped)

ed	/ed/	/d/	/t/

/f/ as in fit

f	ph	gh

/g/ as in game

g	gu	gh

/j/ as in judge

j	g	dge

/k/ as in kick

k | c | ck | ch | que

/l/ as in like

l | le | el | al

/m/ as in mom

m | mb | mn

/n/ as in no

n | kn | gn | pn

/r/ as in rat

r | wr | rh

/s/ as in sun

s | c | sc

/z/ as in zoo

z | s | x